The Maine Coast

A Nature Lover's Guide

Dorcas S. Miller

with illustrations
by Cherie Hunter Day

Published by The East Woods Press
in cooperation with the
Maine Audubon Society

The
East Woods
Press

To Dad, who corrected my spelling.

Copyright© 1979 by Fast & McMillan Publishers, Inc.
First Printing.

Library of Congress Cataloging in Publication Data

Miller, Dorcas S   1949—
   The Maine coast.

   Bibliography: p.
   Includes index.
   1. Natural history—Maine. 2. Coastal ecology—Maine. 3. Maine—Description and travel—Guidebooks. I. Title.
QH105.M2M54   500.9741   79-10290
ISBN 0-914788-12-4

Cover photograph courtesy of Maine State Development Office.
Design and typography by Raven Type.
Printed in the United States of America by The George Banta Company.

East Woods Press Books
Fast & McMillan Publishers, Inc.
820 East Boulevard
Charlotte, NC 28203

About the Author

Dorcas Miller writes in whatever spare time she can find. She holds a Master of Education degree from the University of Massachusetts. Her many experiences as instructor of outdoor education include the Minnesota and Texas Outward Bound schools and Maine Reach, a program for high school seniors and graduates which stresses field experiences. She has also served as an outdoor education outreach coordinator for Maine schools.

Somewhere along the way, Dorcas found time to write *The Healthy Trail Food Book*, which fills a need for people who want to eat simple and healthy food while on the trail.

About the Artist

Cherie Hunter Day is a free lance artist specializing in biological illustration. Her degree is in biology, and her experience includes coordinating art projects for scientific publications. She has won several fine arts awards for her outstanding work.

Contents

List of Illustrations

Foreword

Many have expressed to me their concern that information and publicity about the natural features of Maine will lead to the overuse and abuse of these very special places. The very attractiveness of Maine's unique areas often means that our most fragile and wild places feel increasing pressure from man's presence. Ironically, those of us who care the most about our natural environment could be the cause of its compromise through overuse.

Thus, it is with some trepidation that nature lovers share their experiences, thoughts, and secret places. Many suggest that our best way to protect Maine's unique natural areas is to discourage any information about these places. Unfortunately, this approach offers only a very short-term protection. If use does increase, there is no mechanism to control overuse.

Maine's destiny as a place to recharge the spirits of those from our urban areas was set irrevocably when the first rusticators left Boston and New York in the 1890s to settle summer colonies at Bar Harbor, Kennebunkport and Camden. People will always be coming to Maine in increasing numbers as our population grows. It is something which must be accepted and controlled, for it cannot be otherwise.

Often the very lack of information about our state results in the crowding of visitors in only a few well-publicized coastal areas. Mount Desert Island, Old Orchard Beach and Monhegan Island are but three examples of areas threatened by overuse. However, Maine has hundreds of other islands and miles of coastline that get comparatively no use. The problem here is not the lack of places to visit; it is that people don't know where to go. They end up at the few well-publicized tourist attractions, to the detriment of those areas.

There are several ways in which we can respond to these increasing demands on our beautiful state. First, we can try to instill in others a concern for Maine's magnificent environment. Those who know and love Maine are our best hope to build a coalition to fight to prevent its exploitation. This cannot be achieved, however, by secrecy. We need to show others the vision of Maine we seek to protect. Secondly, we must encourage people to visit new places in our state, so that the pressures on the few over-trampled and over-visited areas can be reduced and controlled.

Dorcas Miller's *The Maine Coast—A Nature Lover's Guide* is a good beginning in the strategy for conserving Maine. It is, first, a concise handbook on the natural forces—climate, geology, biology—that shape Maine. Those who read this book will develop a keen understanding of how environmental and cultural forces have shaped the natural history of Maine.

The Maine Coast is also a fine roadmap to the places where Maine's natural spirit comes nearest to the surface. The coastal places described here in this book are as fine a vision of Maine as are likely to be found in print anywhere. Those who use it will find a little-seen but vastly rewarding side of Maine.

I can only ask one favor of you, the reader of this book. Enjoy Maine's spirit and its environment, but leave it intact for the others who will have the same need as you for contact with the wind, the sea and the coast of Maine.

William Ginn
Executive Director, Maine Audubon Society

Preface

Between Kittery and Lubec lies a most remarkable stretch of coast. Formed by the primal movements of drifting continents, shaped by mountain-building episodes and erosion, scoured by waves of ice which retreated but 12,000 years ago, Maine's shoreline is a necklace of beaches, salt marshes, and rocky headlands. Its natural history is a complex and fascinating saga, a story which is told and retold daily at the edge of the ocean.

The book is written for those who delight in listening to the story . . . people who stop to watch a soaring hawk . . . people who look for prints in freshly fallen snow . . . people who feel the pulse of life as birds migrate south for the winter and return north for the summer. It is designed for the broad range of people who enjoy nature—bird watchers, amateur ecologists, hikers and cross-country skiers, artists, and professional naturalists.

The Maine Coast—A Nature Lover's Guide is organized so that it can be used by individuals with different needs and interests, those who want specific details and those who are generally interested in ecology. Section I introduces Maine's natural history; chapters on geology and history set the stage. Wildlife chapters follow, describing the common birds, mammals, and marine life. Five ecosystem chapters—forest, salt marsh, rocky shore, sand beach, and freshwater wetlands—introduce specific plant and animal communities. The first half of the book is for armchair reading as well as in-the-field reference. What birds and plants are found in Maine's salt marshes? How are sand beaches formed? What effect did the glaciers have on later ecology? The answers to these questions provide basic knowledge of coastal natural history and lead to the second half of the book.

Section II describes over eighty areas of interest which are open to the public. General concepts become more tangible when applied to specific places. What history lies behind the rock formations at Pemaquid Point? What particular beach features can be seen at Popham Beach? What birds migrate through Merrymeeting Bay?

Many of the places listed are state or town parks which are officially open during the summer and free for use the rest of the year. The "off" season is often the best time to investigate—during fall and spring migrations, after a sprinkling of snow has caught the tracks of fox and deer, when visitors are fewer and further between. Not all of these areas are isolated or entirely natural, especially along the southern coast. Developed sites which retain significant natural features have been included nevertheless, for small nearby places are as important as distant "untouched" areas.

Throughout the book, reference is made to birds and mammals usually seen in an area. "Common" indicates that the animal is regularly seen in the proper habitat and that large numbers are reported every year. "Uncommon" means that small numbers are reported each year. Either birds are found in only a few localities or few are seen in the correct habitat during breeding season. "Residents" may be seen year-round while "migrants" usually appear in season, although the season may differ from species to species. In some cases, birds are common at one time of the year and uncommon at another—and not seen at all for the other months.

The major glaring omission in the text is a discussion of coastal islands. Simply there is too much to talk about in Maine. Site descriptions have been limited to areas accessible by car and by foot. Information concerning ferrys to Monhegan, Isle au Haut, Vinal Haven, North Haven, the Casco Bay Islands, and other Maine coast islands is available through local chambers of commerce. Much of the general ecology of the mainland of course applies to the islands.

At several points, the text describes unusual and uncommon species. This material has been included only after much thought. What is the better way to protect something: to keep it secret or to educate the public about its existence? If least tern nesting areas are specified, will visitors rush forward to see an unusual species or maintain a healthy distance in order to protect the birds? Trusting that education is a wiser course than secrecy (which is accompanied by unknowing damage) the writer has not excluded these areas from the text.

But regardless of whether a plant is rare or common, whether a place is wild or developed, the primary method of preserving Maine's natural areas is to follow the nature lover's code: take photographs instead of plants, leave footprints instead of paper, and enjoy the beauty of the earth.

Acknowledgments

Many individuals willingly shared resources and reviewed this manuscript. Hank Tyler from the Critical Areas Program, Ken Fink and Bruce Nelson from the Ira C. Darling Center, and Woodrow Thompson from the Maine Geological Survey were especially helpful. Bob Rothe, Acadia National Park; Steve Katona, Allied Whale; Phil Conkling, Critical Areas Program; Bill Ginn, Maine Audubon Society; and Don Newberg, Bowdoin College Geology Department, also reviewed chapters and weeded out errors.

A special thanks is due to the students and staff of Maine Reach in Wiscasset, where I instructed for three years. The focus of the program is Maine itself. We traveled throughout the state, from Kittery to Allagash, from Eastport to Rangeley, in our shared investigations of the ecology, social studies, and environmental issues of Maine.

The Maine Coast
A Nature Lover's Guide

The Bedrock Foundation

Plate tectonics, lithosphere, aesthenosphere, orogeny. Of all the disciplines in the natural sciences, geology is perhaps the most formidable to the amateur ecologist. It is relatively easy to identify a tree, to observe the creatures in a tide pool. But to identify rocks, pick out land forms, and understand the sequence of events which led to their creation seems a much greater challenge. Yet geology has profoundly influenced both the natural and human history of the coast of Maine. Each succeeding chapter in this book refers to the bedrock foundation and glacial sculpting. The following sketch of Maine coast geology aims at providing a framework for understanding the ancient and far-reaching workings of the earth, in order to set the stage for later developments.

Plate Tectonics

Most geologists agree that the earth's outer layer, the lithosphere, is composed of eight large and several small "plates" which float on a molten interior, the aesthenosphere. Like pieces of wood drifting in a whirlpool, these plates have bumped into each other and floated apart many times. But unlike driftwood, the tectonic plates can slide one under the other, bend, rumple, and change their surface form. Also, molten rock from the aesthenosphere can well up and harden, creating new bedrock on the edges of the plates.

Scientists believe that 560 million years ago the North American tectonic plate and the African plate drifted apart. Magma welled into the rift from below and water filled the basin. A new ocean was created. At the same time, forces of erosion played across the continents, carrying tons of sediments to the edge of the plates and into the newly formed ocean. A thick layer of sediments—as much as 20,000 feet in some places—accumulated.

Four hundred and fifty million years ago, the North American and European plates drifted toward each other, pushing ocean floor under

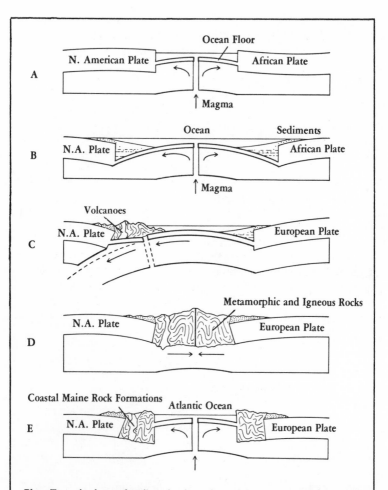

Plate Tectonic theory describes the formation of the rock formations on the Maine coast: (A) 570 million years ago magma wells up through rift, pushing plates apart and forming ocean floor; an ocean is created. (B) Sea floor spreading continues, widening ocean; eroded sentiments from inland accumulate along continental margins. (C) Taconic Orogeny: 500 million years ago North American and European plate drift together, closing the ocean. Ocean floor is forced under North American plate, creating volcanoes. (D) Acadian Orogeny: 390 million years ago the ocean is closed. Margins of two plates are folded and injected with magma from below. Heat and pressure change sedimentary rocks to metamorphic rocks. (E) Continents begin to spread again, forming new ocean floor and the Atlantic Ocean. Ocean floor spreading continues today.

North America. The ocean floor did not slide easily and a series of volcanoes rose along the line of disturbance. These volcanoes spewed ashes and debris which inter-layered with continually accumulating sediments.

As the European plate collided with the chain of volcanoes and later with the North American plate, great changes took place. The edges of the plates folded and cracked. Rocks were forced upward into huge mountains. Magma welled through the cracks and crevices. Heat and pressure changed the structure of vast expanses of sedimentary rocks which lay on the continental shelf. The once evenly layered sedimentary rocks of the coast were crushed and crumpled.

Taconic and Acadian Orogenies

"Oro" means mountain and "genesis" means to be born. Orogeny, then is the process by which mountains are created. Two sequences of mountain building are documented in New England during the closure of the ocean. The Taconic Orogeny occurred 450 million years ago when the European plate piled into the volcanic chain. The Acadian Orogeny followed when the European plate joined the North American plate 390 million years ago.

The continental plates continued to shift. Africa subsequently drifted into North America and Europe, and then all three plates separated. But the rock record indicates an interesting aspect of plate tectonics. When the plates separated, they did so along new lines. Trilobite fossils found in parts of Maine resemble those found in Europe and Africa rather than the Pacific trilobite fossils found in the rest of North America. Apparently parts of North America were once within the realm of Europe and Africa. Likewise, a section of western Africa contains Pacific trilobite fossils and was once a part of North America.

By 70 million years ago, the plates had separated to the extent that the Atlantic was a major ocean and the continents were in the approximate positions shown on today's map. Continual erosion since the orogenies has worn down the huge mountains which stood along the Maine coast and across New England. The remnants of these mountains—modified by glaciation—constitute the present-day New England Upland.

The migration of plates has not ceased, however. The rift in the Atlantic Ocean continues to ooze magma from within the earth along the mid-Atlantic Ridge as the continents split farther apart. The North American plate drifts westward more than one inch each year, about six feet during the course of an average human lifetime. The geologic processes which shaped the oceans and continents during the last 700 million years continue to do so and invite speculation as to the course of the future.

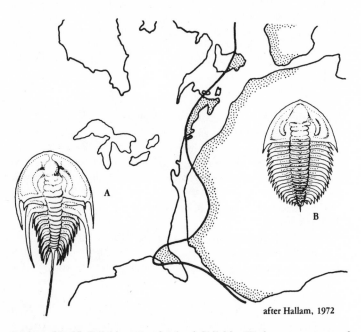

after Hallam, 1972

Realms of Pacific Trilobite (A) and Atlantic Trilobite (B) show arrangement of continental lands during Acadian Orogeny 390 million years ago.

The Rock Record

The theories of plate tectonics are based on evidence left in rocks—the rock record. Mt. Desert Island is an excellent site to study one such record, for bedrock is widely exposed there. Although the complete geologic history of Mt. Desert is much more complex than the simplification presented here, the following example serves to explain the processes which affected the entire coast.

If three very deep wells were drilled near Bar Harbor, the rock samples from the drill holes might indicate the vertical relationships between rock types shown on the next page:

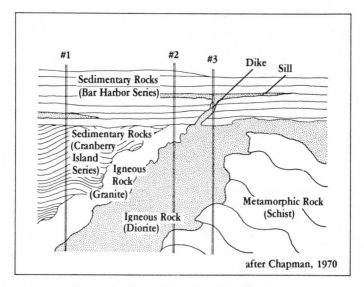

Cross-sectional map of Mt. Desert Island bedrock.

A whole series of core drillings would produce a fuller picture.

On the surface lie sedimentary rocks, rocks composed of loose sediments that later compacted and hardened. The "Bar Harbor" sedimentary rocks are siltstones, conglomerates, and volcanic ash, formed from silt, small rocks and ash. Below the Bar Harbor Series lies more sedimentary rock, but of a different nature. The "Cranberry Island" Series, named after nearby islands, is composed of volcanic ash and rock fragments.

Igneous rocks—those which formed when molten material from the earth's interior came to or near the surface, cooled, and hardened—underlie the sedimentary rocks. Granite and diorite are both coarse-grained igneous rocks, indicating that the parent magma cooled slowly, allowing relatively large crystals to form. (Lava, on the other hand, cools much more quickly because it is exposed to the earth's atmosphere; the rock produced is quite fine-grained.) Because magma can flow into cracks and force its way between sheets of sedimentary rocks, particular formations can result. In drill hole #2, diorite is sandwiched between layers of Bar Harbor sedimentary rocks. The diorite is actually a "sill," a sheet of igneous rock that is parallel to the surrounding rock layers. Likewise, igneous rock which forces its way into a cross-cutting crack forms a wall or "dike."

19

Beneath the igneous rocks lies schist, a metamorphic rock. Metamorphic rocks are sedimentary and igneous rocks which have literally changed form ("meta" means changed and "morphic" means form) due to heat and pressure. The intense pressure created when tectonic plates collided and the heat released by flowing magma changed most of Maine's sedimentary rocks into metamorphic rocks. Schist was formed when shale, a sedimentary rock composed of clay particles, was subjected to great heat and pressure.

Interpreting the Data

Two axioms of geology help decipher the rock pattern indicated by the drillings. First, if a series of sedimentary rocks has not been overturned, the uppermost rocks are the youngest and the lowermost are the oldest. Therefore the schist is oldest, being a metamorphosed sedimentary rock. Then the Cranberry Island rocks formed on the surface of the schist and the Bar Harbor Series was deposited last. Second, an igneous rock is younger than any rock it intrudes. Diorite, which has forced its way through the schist and Cranberry Island Series and into the Bar Harbor Series, is younger than the sedimentary and metamorphic rocks. Other drillings in the Bar Harbor area indicate that the granite is even younger.

A knowledge of how the rocks were created, combined with their relative ages enables us to reconstruct the following geologic history. First, clay particles, deposited when the area was covered by a shallow sea, built up and eventually formed shale. The region was subjected to heat and pressure. Evenly layered beds of shale became the uneven beds of schist. A period of erosion followed, wearing away much of the schist.

Next, a layer of fine ash and rock fragments (the Cranberry Island Series) was laid down by volcanoes, the same volcanoes which were created when the European tectonic plate pushed ocean floor under the North American plate. This volcanic "tuff" as it is called was also subjected to deformation, producing a wavy appearance. More erosion followed. The Bar Harbor Series—siltstones, conglomerates, and more volcanic ash—was deposited last.

During the Acadian Orogeny, dioritic magma invaded the area. It forced a passage through the schist and tuff and into the Bar Harbor rocks, forming sills and dikes. A second wave of intruding magma, with somewhat different mineral composition, worked between the diorite and tuff. Over the intervening 350 million years, thousands of feet of rock have been eroded, exposing the bedrock which is seen today.

This reconstruction of the geologic history of Mt. Desert Island is similar to the history all along the coast, though there are many complexities and individual exceptions. Generally, sedimentary rocks formed from eroded materials deposited along the edge of the North American tectonic plate. These rocks were changed by the heat and pressure generated during the two mountain-building periods, the Taconic and Acadian Orogenies. The deformed metamorphic rocks were interjected with magma, creating bodies of granite, diorite, and other igneous rocks. The coastal mountains were gradually eroded, producing an area of less topographic relief.

Further Reading and Reference

Continents Adrift and Continents Aground, readings from *Scientific American* with an introduction by J. Tuzo Wilson (W.H. Freeman and Company, 1976.) A technical yet fascinating series of articles concerning plate tectonics.

The Geology of Acadia National Park by Carleton A. Chapman (The Chatham Press, Inc., 1970.) Readable description of the bedrock and glacial geology of Mount Desert Island, including site descriptions.

A Guide to New England's Landscape, by Neil Jorgensen (Barre Publishers, 1971.) An excellent account of bedrock geology for the entire New England region. Very readable.

Maps of the bedrock geology of Maine may be obtained from the Maine Geological Survey, Department of Conservation, Augusta, Maine 04333. Write for index and prices.

Influence of the Glaciers

The very last chapter of coastal geologic history began about one million years ago and is known as the Ice Age, or more technically Pleistocene Epoch. A variety of complex factors triggered a change in the earth's climate and more snow fell than melted in the colder regions of the Northern Hemisphere. As snow accumulated, its weight compressed the lower layers into a thick, viscous mass of ice. The ice flowed like a river into valleys and lowlands, growing in size, until it finally enveloped mountains and covered the surface of the land.

At least four separate ice sheets advanced and receded over parts of Canada and the northern United States. The last sheet blanketed half of the North American continent. It flowed southeastward over the eroded New England hills, entering Maine about 20,000 years ago. At its center near Hudson's Bay, the glacier was two miles thick. Maine, located on the perimeter, lay under a thinner burden of ice about one mile deep. The ocean level dropped 200-300 feet below the present level, exposing a large strip of continental shelf to the steadily moving ice. The glacier reached as far east and south as Georges Bank, Cape Cod and Long Island. The North American tectonic plate, floating on a molten interior, sank beneath the tremendous weight of the ice.

When the world-wide climate warmed, the glacier began to recede. The ocean flooded the still-depressed land, reaching over forty miles inland at its maximum incursion 12,800 years ago. Initially the sea was in contact with the glacier, but the ice margin soon receded from the submerged coastal lowland. Meltwater streams then followed the major valleys—Androscoggin, Kennebec, Penobscot—to the Atlantic. With the heavy load of ice diminishing, the earth began to rebound and the edge of the ocean moved southeastward past the present coastline.

However, as the polar ice caps continued to melt, more water was added to the ocean's reservoir. Worldwide sea level began rising and has continued to rise. In Maine, the increase averages two inches each century.

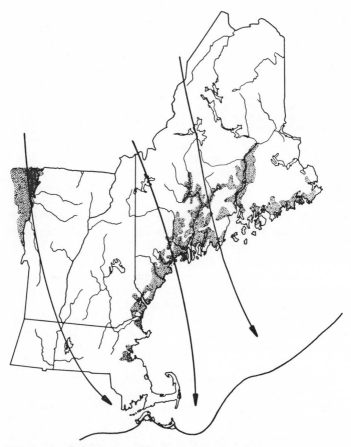

Map showing farthest extent of ice (⟵) during last glaciation and extent of marine flooding during late-glacial times (dark areas).

Glacial Features

Although it little affected the bedrock foundation, glaciation had a major effect on the landscape. Many of these features are visible in Maine. *Glacial till*, rock debris eroded and carried in the ice, was left haphazardly when the ice melted and now lies in a thin layer over the countryside. Bouldery till was especially troublesome to settlers who harvested crops of rock in addition to corn and wheat from their New England farms. The stone walls which mark their fields stand as further evidence to the generous helping of rocks left by the glacier.

Occasionally the ice carried large boulders a great distance and deposited them either singly or in boulder fields. These *erratics* are clearly of different rock than the bedrock on which they lie. Huge erratics may be seen on the South Bubble and along the South Ridge of Cadillac Mountain on Mt. Desert Island.

The island also contains *U-shaped valleys* which were scooped out by flowing ice. In some places, ice removed as much as 500 feet of rock. Water-carved valleys have a characteristic V-shape, while glacially scoured valleys like those on Mt. Desert are rounded to a smooth U. The only true fjord in the United States, Somes Sound, is a deeply scoured valley which was subsequently drowned by the rising ocean.

Some Maine mountains show an asymmetrical shape which resulted from glacial grinding and plucking. Their north and northwest sides are smoothed, while their south and southeast slopes are steep and sharp in profile. This *stoss and lee topography* was produced as the ice scoured the stoss (upstream) sides of the mountains and detached blocks of rock from the lee (downstream) sides.

Eskers are common features in Maine. When meltwater streams flowed in tunnels through glacial ice, they carried a load of stones and sand. After the ice melted, these sediments lay exposed as long, win-

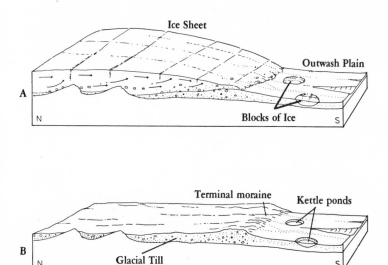

after Strahler, 1966

A Ice Sheet covers the land.
B Ice has melted, leaving glacial features.

ding ridges that run northwest to southeast, perpendicular to the edge of the glacier. Eskers are often mined for sand and gravel. The Whaleback and Horseback in Aurora are examples of these features.

Moraines were created when rock debris carried by the ice and meltwater streams (till, sand, and gravel) was brought forward to the outer edge of the glacier and accumulated as ridges. These ridges formed parallel to the edge of the glacier. Large moraines like Cape Cod, Martha's Vineyard, Nantucket and Long Island were created when the glacier was stationary for an extended time. Another large end moraine was deposited on Georges Bank beyond Maine's present shoreline. Much smaller "washboard" moraines were left as the ice made small pauses in its retreat. Moraine ridges may provide viable areas for domestic sewage-disposal systems along the coast, where the surrounding material commonly is impermeable bedrock or clay.

As meltwater streams emerged from the ice, they carried a heavy load of sediments that were eventually deposited, resulting in a variety of landforms (such as deltas, kames and outwash plains). *Outwash plains* greatly influenced the southern coast, where long beaches were formed from sandy outwash that was moved about by wind and water in postglacial time.

The myriad *lakes, ponds, and kettleholes* which dot Maine's surface are also signs of the glacier. Insulated by sand and gravel that had buried them, great chunks of ice sometimes lingered for centuries. When they finally melted, depressions (kettleholes) were created, many of which are now occupied by ponds. Others have been partly or entirely filled with bog vegetation, while still others are completely dry.

Further Reading and Reference

A Geologist's View of Cape Cod by Arthur N. Strahler (The Natural History Press, 1966.) Excellent account of glaciation in New England and specifically Cape Cod. Very readable.

A Guide to New England's Landscape by Neil Jorgensen (Barre Publishers, 1971.) Good section on glacial geology and formations which may be seen in New England.

Maps of glacial and marine deposits in Maine may be obtained from the Maine Geological Survey, Department of Conservation, Augusta, Maine 04333. Write for index and prices.

History and Natural Resources

Maine is relatively long on geological history and short on human history. Glacial ice erased all traces of any prehistoric man who may have hunted the wooly mammoth and mastadons of New England. The earliest artifacts date from 3000-4000 B.C. Stone implements decorated with carvings, spear points, stone knives, and fire-making utensils belonged to paleo-Indians who roamed the coastal forests for game and later developed more stable settlements based on fishing and agriculture. Artifacts have been discovered at Ellsworth Falls, Brassua, Blue Hill, Passadumkeag, and Alton. The Indians are called Maritime Boreal Archaic or, more commonly, the "Red Paint People" in honor of their burial customs. They gathered iron oxide—at some effort, for they went to the slopes of Mount Katahdin—and mixed it with clay to make a red ochre which they smeared in the graves.

No legends of the Red Paint People are carried into the oral history of later Indians. The next thread of habitation appears between 80 and 350 A.D. in the form of huge oyster and clam shell mounds. The "Oyster Shell Men" lived in over 750 areas along the coast, leaving compost from many years of feasts as proof. Some of the middens reach 400 feet in length and are more than 20 feet deep.

The Abenaki Nation

The Abenakis, a branch of the Alonquins, were the next people to inhabit the coast. They called Maine "the land of the dawn" (meaning the east) and are known as the Dawn People. The Androscoggins, Kennebecs, Penobscots, Passamaquoddies, and others were all distinct tribes in the Abenaki, or Wabenaki nation. Although they spoke a similar language, each tribe had individual customs and home areas, as their names indicate.

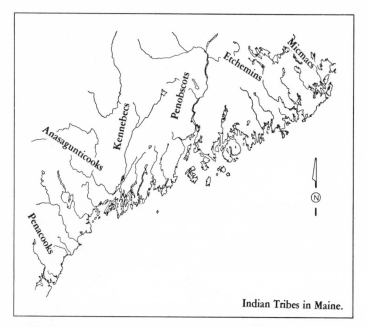

Indian Tribes in Maine.

The Abenakis were peace-loving farmers who lived along the coast and shores of larger rivers and lakes. They grew beans, squash, corn and pumpkins; gathered wild berries and fruits; made maple syrup; and supplemented their diet with game meat and fish. They developed a democratic government and a written language, using the inner bark of the birch tree for paper. They used birch bark for other things, too. They designed beautiful canoes, some of which could carry two dozen men, and made baskets and utensils.

The Abenaki Nation numbered 3000 at its height. Disease and war decimated the tribes. As settlers bought or stole their lands, the Indians were pushed onto reservations in Old Town, Princeton, and Eastport. Today about 1000 Indians—primarily Passamaquoddies and Penobscots—remain in Maine.

The political and legal arena has changed considerably. Federal court decisions favor the Abenaki claim to their ancestral hunting grounds, a huge tract of land east of the Penobscot River. The case is complicated, but is based on the trustee relationship that the United States govern-ment holds with all Indian nations. To protect Indians from unscrupulous land dealers, Congress passed the Non-Intercourse Act in 1794 which stated that the Federal Government must ratify any treaty between Indians and non-Indians. By custom, however, Indians of the

13 colonies were treated as wards of the state and in many instances the treaties were not federally approved. In effect, the treaties by which the Abenakis gave up most of their aboriginal lands were never legal and only in the 1970s have these issues been brought to light.

Indian artifact.

Early Explorers

But neither the Indians nor the white sailors and explorers who first came to the coast of North America had any inkling of what was to come. The first visitors were probably Viking voyagers from Norway and Greenland. Alleged Viking markings have been discovered on Monhegan Island and on the Outer Heron Islands, and there is some speculation that Thorvald, Leif Erikson's brother, met his death on Mt. Desert in a skirmish with the natives. Historians do know for certain that the Vikings explored Nova Scotia in the early 11th century, and that they continued south along the coast is quite likely.

French and English seamen began exploring the "New World" almost 500 years later. The Cabots sailed to Maine several times in the 1490s. Giovanni da Verrazano mapped the area in 1524 for the King of France. Captain Bartholomew Gosnold visited in 1602. Martin Pring sailed a year later. These initial adventurers looked not for settlement sites, but for gold and a route to the Orient. They found a stern landscape, but what lay beyond the rocky shore and tall pines, no one knew. Perhaps it was the splendor of the Indies.

Meanwhile, fishermen from France, Portugal, Spain, and England were finding splendor of a much different sort. Cod, haddock, mackerel, perch, herring, and other species abounded in the North Atlantic. Like the Vikings, the fishermen kept no records—in fact, they kept the lucrative sites confidential—but when Champlain sailed into the Penobscot in 1604, it is written that he met with a fisherman who had already made 42 trips to Maine. By 1550, over 300 sailing vessels were hauling fish from the North Atlantic seas, and many were put into the calm harbors nearby to dry fish and take on fresh water.

British and French Settlement

In the 1600s, Britain and France began simultaneous efforts to control the northeast coast. The English concentrated on Massachusetts and southern Maine, while the French moved south from the St. Lawrence. A conflict between an English sea captain and Jesuit priests on Mt. Desert Island marked the beginning of a long and bloody feud between the two nations, a conflict of attacks and reprisals, broken treaties, revenge and burned settlements. Towns were devastated, rebuilt, and destroyed again. France gained the help of the Indians, but no one ever won in these years of terror. One war followed another: King Phillip's War, King William's War, the War of the Austrian Succession, the French and Indian War. Maine lay between the French and English territories, claimed by both great nations who were engaged in an even greater struggle for world supremacy.

Maine was a prize and England won. With the Peace of Paris in 1763, France abandoned claim to the vast timberlands, excellent deep water harbors, and potential fur trade. Attention and energy was at last turned from war and toward exploiting the timber, pelts, fishing grounds, and agricultural resources.

Exploitation is an appropriate word, for England's policy dictated that the colonies supply the mother country with raw materials. Mills and factories in Britain turned out finished goods, which were then sold to the colonies. Family operations in Maine—sawmills, grist mills, tanneries, copper works, small textile mills—served only local needs.

Revolutionary War

The Revolutionary War changed that balance of goods, but only after another long and bitter struggle. Although fighting centered to the south, two incidents are of note in Maine history books. Both were failures. In 1775 Benedict Arnold led an expedition up the Kennebec River and into Canada to assault Quebec City. The troops, including a good number of Maine men, were harassed by floods, poorly constructed boats, spoiled food, treachery, desertion, and sickness. Arnold arrived with one-third of his original number, fought gallantly, but was defeated by the British. "Benedict Arnold" may mean "traitor" to most Americans, but Maine has reserved a special admiration for Arnold's boldness and courage against superior forces, as told in Kenneth Roberts' classic rendition of the expedition, *Arundel*.

The second defeat, even more dismal for its lack of heroism, occurred when American leaders decided to attack the British stronghold at Castine. Poorly equipped and trained troops were sent under the direction of Lt. Col. Paul Revere. Despite the advantage of seige and superior numbers, the Americans could not penetrate the defense. When confronted by a British relief squadron, they turned tail, sailed up the

Penobscot, scudded the ships, and made for home. This embarrassing episode did render some benefits—in the long run. Colonial artifacts and ship timbers are now being excavated by divers and restored by the Maine State Museum.

The "Golden Era"

The small-town economy of the early 1800s rapidly blossomed into Maine's "Golden Era" in the middle of the century. The state had seemingly limitless timber resources when wood was the key to the economy, as oil is today. Ship building flourished in every coastal town. An average of 250 wooden vessels slid down the ways every year between 1820 and 1860. By 1855, one-third of the U.S. tonnage was Maine built. Waldoboro, Bath, and Portland grew into major commercial towns with a cosmopolitan population, for Maine vessels traded with every port in the world.

In the same manner, Maine dominated the fishing industry. Shortly before the Civil War, Maine had more registered fishing vessels on the seas than any state in the union and placed second in annual value of catch. Other industries sprang up. By 1860 textile mills along the southern coast employed several thousand people. Timber, ship-building, textiles, trade, and fishing provided ample jobs and economic opportunity.

Shipbuilding, Bath, 1800s

Only farming decreased during this time of expansion. Maine's glacial soil is thin and often poor. Consistent crop failures and severe winters in the early part of the century had infected farmers with "Ohio fever," and over 15,000 families forsook their hard earned plots for the better land and warmer climate in the mid-west.

But the Golden Age ended. The Civil War and the advent of iron-clad ships doomed the era of wood. Ship-building declined and overseas trade moved to other ports. Maine slid from the limelight as quickly as its ships once slid from their ways.

Today's Economy

Maine's present economy depends heavily on resource-based industry. Paper, wood, and furniture manufacturing have a total value of over 1.2 billion dollars yearly. Potatoes, poultry, and fishing reap the bounty of land and sea. The open country, picturesque lands, stunning coastline, and fresh salt air lure visitors from all parts of the country and provide 300 million dollars per year.

But inevitably, the limitless resources were discovered to be limited. Industrial wastes polluted the Kennebec, Androscoggin, and Penobscot Rivers. Abundant supplies of cod dwindled to the extent that a ban was placed on cod fishing. Houses, business, and industry crowded the coastline, defacing the beauty which had orginally invited development. Maine grew without plan or thought.

The trend was not irreversible. The state passed the strictest environmental laws in the nation. As a result, salmon are now returning to the rivers. The Kennebec River has water clean enough to swim in. Coastal zoning and land management have replaced haphazard development. Open burning at dumps has been outlawed. Many unique regions of the state have been preserved as public land. With continued vigilance, Maine can restore damaged areas and use—rather than abuse—its valuable natural environment.

Further Reading and Reference

Arundel by Kenneth Roberts (Doubleday & Co., Inc., 1930)

Kennebec, Cradle of America by Robert P.T. Coffin (Farrar and Rinehart, 1937). A delightful telling of Maine's history.

Timber Resources of Maine by Roland Ferguson and Neal Kingsley (U.S.D.A. Forest Service Resource Bulletin NE-26, 1972). Summary of Maine's timber resources, contains many tables and charts.

Birds

Whoever has heard the lilting of a song sparrow, or watched the courtship flight of a woodcock, or sat quietly by an estuary as an osprey dove for fish; whoever knows spring by the return of Canada geese and marks fall by when they go south; whoever faithfully fills the feeder with sunflower seeds and keeps track of the winter visitors—these people know the joys that birds can bring. Bird watching is more than gazing through binoculars and checking off names on a "life list." Rachael Carson once discussed the effects of man's intervention in natural processes and asked, "What would happen if there were no birds?" The answer, in *Silent Spring*, was sobering. Indeed, birds are indicators of the health of the environment and they add immeasurable happiness to everyday living.

Over 300 birds frequent Maine's coast and woodlands, far too many to catalog in this section. Instead, birds frequently seen in a particular environment—forest, rocky shore, beach, salt marsh, freshwater wetland—have been included in each ecosystem chapter. One of the easiest ways to begin birding is to become familiar with bird habitats, as the list of possible species is smaller and more manageable. The lists included in this book are based on *Annotated Checklist of Maine Birds* by Peter D. Vickery.

Identification

Size, shape, behavior, color, and songs are all useful field marks for identifying birds. If possible, compare a new bird with a common species nearby, such as a robin, a crow, or a herring gull in order to judge its size. In some cases, size is the major point of identification. Otherwise, downy and hairy woodpeckers look quite the same, and sharp-shinned and Cooper's hawks are difficult to differentiate.

The shape of a bird—its build, posture, legs, tail, bill, head, silhouette—tells much about the bird's habits as well as its name. Seed

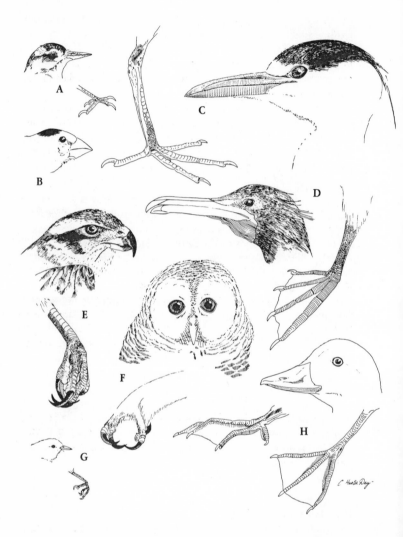

Bills and feet illustrate different lives of birds. (A) Hairy woodpecker; (B) Evening grosbeak; (C) Black-crowned night heron; (D) Double-crested cormorant; (E) Goshawk; (F) Barred owl; (G) Myrtle warbler; (H) American scoter duck.

eaters, such as sparrows, finches, and buntings, have stubby, short bills. Cardinals and grosbeaks have thicker bills more adapted to splitting larger, harder seed casings. Crossbills (the name gives it away) specialize in picking seeds from conifer cones. Warblers and wrens have thin, pointed bills for nabbing insects, while birds of prey use hooked bills for ripping flesh.

Flight patterns are keys to the recognition of different species. The kingfisher, sparrow hawk, rough-legged hawk, marsh hawk, osprey, and terns hover when hunting. Woodpeckers, nuthatches, and goldfinches have an undulating flight. Sparrows and robins fly with even wingbeats. Eagles, ospreys, buteo hawks, and sometimes gulls are known for soaring. Diving ducks like the common goldeneye, bufflehead, mergansers, and scaups flap along the water when taking off or landing, whereas teal and black ducks (which feed in ponds and marshes without a "runway") lift right out of the water.

Some behaviors are so particular that they are give-aways. For example, the double-crested cormorant does not oil its feathers like other water birds and so it must sit with its wings outstretched to let them dry in the sun—much like hanging out the wash.

The common names of birds often indicate distinctive color patterns. The black-backed gull, ruby-throated hummingbird, yellow-shafted flicker, green-winged teal, goldfinch, rose-breasted grosbeak and harlequin duck tell of the rainbow colors revealed in bird plumages and aid in identification.

Many people find bird songs hard to recognize, but some are so catchy that they are easy to remember. "Chick-a-dee, dee, dee" "pe-wee," "phoe-be," "whip-poor-will" present no problems. Other birds have songs which sound like a phrase in English. The hoot of the barred owl resembles, "Who cooks for you, who cooks for you," while the white-throated sparrow whistles a song like, "Oh, sweet Canada, Canada, Canada."

Roadside Birding

Although bird watching from a car does not sound as appealing as tracking herons and egrets far from the rumble of a highway, roadside birding offers some advantages. Maine's coast has an abundance of country roads which skirt a variety of ecosystems—woods, bays, rocky shore, salt marshes—and the lower speed limit is more conducive to identification. The automobile can be used as a blind, for birds which will fly at human movement are accustomed to cars.

Moreover, many birds are attracted to the roadside. Power lines and

Herring gull fledgling.

telephone poles serve as resting spots and hunting perches. Frogs, mice and small mammals which try to cross the road are exposed and can easily be caught. Larger animals like skunk and porcupine, unable to avoid cars, become food for scavengers like the crow and bluejay. The heat of the pavement attracts insects, which in turn attracts insect-eaters. And, after a rain, worms are often stranded on the road—a good mouthful for an attentive robin.

Because the ''back road'' is a unique community and does not fit into any of the ecosystem chapters, a list of birds commonly seen on country roads is included here.

Wire sitters
American kestrel
Rock dove (pigeon)
Mourning dove
Tree swallow
Bank swallow
Barn swallow
Purple martin
Mockingbird
Cedar waxwing
Starling
House sparrow

Red-winged blackbird
Common grackle

Fence post sitters
Common nighthawk
Eastern meadowlark
Red-winged blackbird

Road kill scavengers
Blue jay
Common crow

Other birds which frequent the roadside

Ring-necked pheasant	Indigo bunting
Common flicker	American goldfinch
Grey catbird	Chipping sparrow
Brown thrasher	Song sparrow
Cardinal	

Equipment for birding is fairly basic; a clean pair of binoculars and an identification book. 8 x 35 (8 is the magnification, 35 is the diameter in millimeters of the front or "objective" lens) are standard binoculars. *Birds of North America* or *Peterson's Field Guide to Birds* are also standard. A small notebook for jotting down species, behavior, and interesting observations helps keep track of what has been seen and serves as a reference to the watcher.

Several organizations lead trips of interest to birders and naturalists. The Maine Audubon Society sponsors over 40 field trips each year, many of them to unique birding areas, and local Audubon chapters also schedule excursions. The National Audubon Society runs summer workshops on Hog Island in Bremen.

The traditional image of bird-watchers as rather stuffy, peculiar people has vanished as bird watching has become a popular pastime. Many individuals who did not know the difference between a robin and a sparrow, who thought that all birds were brown, are now avid watchers who derive great pleasure from observing the comings and goings of these feathered creatures.

Further Reading and Reference

Annotated Checklist of Maine Birds by Peter Vickery (1978)

Birds of North America by Chandler Robins, Bertel Bruun, and Herbert Zim (Golden Press, 1966)

A Field Guide to the Birds by Roger Tory Peterson (Houghton Mifflin Company, 1968)

The Habitat Guide to Birding by Thomas McElroy, Jr. (Alfred A. Knopf, 1974)

Animals of the Land

Most animals are shy, furtive, and silent. Many are nocturnal. You can't keep a mammal list like you can keep a bird list, for the page is dishearteningly empty. But while the animals themselves are hard to spot—most are seen in the glare of headlights at night—their signs are everywhere. With a practiced eye you can see feathers, drops of blood, bones, chewed twigs and bark, holes in the ground and tracks in the snow. They all tell stories about the animals which left them—fascinating stories of predators and prey, of escape or death. Winter is an especially good time to track animals, for prints are preserved in the snow. A bit of sleuthing can provide clues which, pieced together, reveal much about the life and habits of the animals.

Some of the very common coastal mammals are the Eastern chipmunk, red squirrel, white-footed mouse, red fox, white-tail deer, beaver, snowshoe hare, porcupine, striped skunk, and raccoon. Because some mammals show a range of habitat, and because most mammals are not often seen, life history information is grouped in this section rather than being divided into ecosystem chapters.

White-tailed Deer

The white-tailed deer was scarce in Maine's virgin forest. Timber cutting and clearing for farmland stimulated growth of brushy vegetation and young trees, producing prime deer habitat. As a result, the deer population expanded. The current state population is estimated at over 200,000 animals. Ironically, the state issues about that same number of hunting licenses each year. As deer are relatively free of diseases and historical natural predators have been eliminated, hunting is used as a population control as well as a sport. However, a new predator—Eastern coyote—has moved into southern Maine and may hold deer populations in check in the future.

Deer are common in cedar swamps, young spruce forests, fields, and recently logged areas. They feed at night, eating grass in the summer

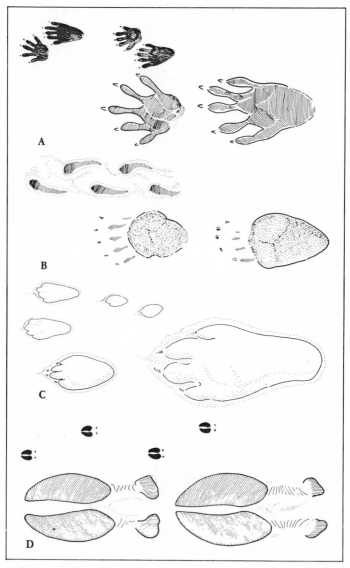

Animal tracks in snow. (A) Raccoon; (B) Porcupine; (C) Snowshoe Hare; (D) Deer.

and switching to the buds of deciduous trees and foliage of evergreens (hemlock and cedar are favorites) in winter. Deer-browsed twigs are easy to identify. The ragged end indicates that it has been chewed with the molars of a deer, as opposed to the sharp clean cut of a hare's incisors.

During the day, deer bed down in protected areas. Ruffled leaves or an area of packed snow underneath protective spruce or fir trees indicate that the animals have taken refuge. Deer scat—dark black pellets with a small point at one end—are also sure clues.

Late winter is a hard time of year. Deer tend to cluster in a yard, a limited area with numerous packed trails. If the region is over-populated, the food supply is quickly consumed, and the animals must rely on fat reserves and food with marginal value. Snow more than 1½ feet deep makes movement difficult and severe browsing in the yard can threaten the health of the vegetation. A long winter with heavy snow can decimate the deer population, as well as the trees and shrubs.

When walking, the deer places its hind foot in the print of the front foot, making a neat trail. In snow, it leaves a two-toed indentation at the base of each print and sometimes makes drag marks between steps.

Snowshoe Hare

The snowshoe hare is an animal of the North. As winter approaches, the shortened day length affects the reproductive cycle, which in turn causes the hare to molt its gray-brown fur. A white coat, good camouflage for the winter, protects the hare from the fox, coyote, mink, great horned owl, goshawk, and lynx. In fact, the abundance of hare and the large number of animals which feed upon it make it a key animal in the northern forest ecosystem.

The hare shows another adaptation to winter, one which is visible in its tracks. Each hind foot has four long toes which spread widely to form a "snowshoe" to stay on top of deep and fluffy snow. Also, the entire foot is well furred, providing additional support. Unlike deer, hares are aided by snow, for they are able to reach more twigs, buds, and bark.

Hares prefer dense stands of young conifers for food and cover and are also found in natural open areas. During the summer they may range over 20 acres, but inclement weather—rain, snow, severe wind—reduces their activity. During the winter they remain in a few acres, becoming very familiar with their runways and paths, giving them a decided advantage over predators which cannot know the area so intimately.

Hares forage at night and by day rest in "forms," hollows in leaves and grass and under shrubs, protected from wind and predators. Their

41

Snowshoe Hare.

slightly flattened, spherical scats, composed of chewed plant material, are found nearby. When food is scarce, it is not uncommon for hares to eat their own scat to gain sustenance from undigested portions. Unlike the cottontail, the young of the hare are born fully furred, have their eyes open, and can hop almost immediately.

Of any track in the wood, snowshoe prints are easiest to identify. The animals leap ahead, hitting the snow with both small front feet and swinging their hind feet forward.

Beaver

The beaver is the largest rodent in North America, weighing 40-60 pounds, but it is nowhere as large as its Ice Age ancestors which grew to be 9 feet long and weighed 800 pounds. With the retreat of the glaciers these giant beavers, along with the mastodons and mammoths, became extinct but gave rise to the smaller animals which today frequent Maine's rivers and streams. The present day beaver almost became extinct, too. Although it was plentiful when the settlers arrived, it was heavily trapped during the 1800s, the fur being prized for fashionable

European hats. Only by reintroduction and strict conservation measures has the species developed a healthy population.

Beaver tracks are rarely seen but dams, lodges, gnawed trees, twigs, and saplings stripped of bark are clear evidence of a nearby family. Beavers eat tender young bark, peeling branches and then using the wood in their dams and lodges. Even if it has food, the animal must continue to chew, for its incisors constantly grow and if they are not worn down, they could grow so large that the beaver could not feed.

A beaver pair begins building its dam in August when the water level is lowest. Trees are placed with the butt end upstream. Rocks, branches, and mud are piled on top until the barrier is water tight, damming the stream to create a pond so deep that it will not freeze in winter. The beaver then has easy access out through his lodge and under the ice to an underwater cache of branches, which keeps the family nourished.

Lodges are built in September, after the dam is finished. The homes are about 15 feet in diameter and 5-6 feet high, and may contain several chambers. Each compartment has two openings, one exit and one entrance. The pair packs the lodge with mud, which freezes into an impenetrable barrier. Only the otter, which can swim into the lodge, poses a threat.

Porcupine

The porcupine is the "odd fellow" of the rodent family. Unlike its speedy and agile relatives, the porcupine is slow and clumsy. When it acquired its armor of quills, it no longer needed to move quickly. But the heavy defense and slow gait are a mixed blessing. Although the animal avoids trouble and backs off when approached, it is unafraid of other animals and is unaware of the power of its most recently evolved predator, the automobile. Most travelers see dead porcupines by the side of the road more often than live ones in the woods.

Fishers are the natural predators of porcupines. When fishers were heavily trapped one hundred years ago, the predator-prey balance changed and the porcupine population blossomed. Although trapping is presently permitted, it is on a limited basis and fishers are more common now than at the turn of the century. More fishers mean less porcupines, and a new balance—resembling the pre-trapping era—is being established.

Porcupines leave three identifiable signs: a tree or den residence, distinctive evidence of feeding, and scats. Their dens in a rock cave or hole in a tree are littered with oval, mustard-brown scats composed of wood fiber. They eat the inner bark, preferably of conifers, but never actually chew on the wood. The gnawed area of a trunk or limb has neat edges, an irregular outline, and many small teeth marks. Often porcupines will chew the tips off hemlock branches, covering the ground below with hemlock fronds and scat.

When attacked, the porcupine curls up, bristles, and becomes a living pincushion. It flips its tail to ward off predators and although the quills cannot be "thrown" they easily detach and the barbed ends become painfully imbedded.

The porcupine leaves alternate pigeon-toed prints. In 6 inches or more of snow, it must plow its way and forms a trough marked by the swish of tail drags.

Striped Skunk

Like the porcupine, the skunk has given up speed and depends heavily on a defense mechanism, in this case well developed scent glands. All weasels have strong glands, but the skunk is by far the winner in an unpleasant smell contest. "Mephitis," its scientific name, is Latin for "bad odor." It can spray up to 20 feet and accurately directs the fluid within 5-10 feet. The skunk is not aggressive and, given the option, will always retreat. But it too has not yet adapted to a change in habitat and is often killed when crossing highways.

The skunk forages in late afternoon, evening, and through the night, usually within 1½ miles of its den. Its omnivorous diet includes insects, mice, shrews, ground squirrels, young rabbits, bird eggs and carrion as well as plants. It uses almost any cavity for a den—an abandoned burrow, a hollow log, a rock crevice, or under buildings. Few animals can stomach the smell, so bobcats and birds of prey (which have developed keen eyesight at the expense of their sense of smell) are the chief predators. The great horned owl, which is little affected by the odor, delights in skunk for dinner.

Skunks travel in a meandering, foraging pattern. In snow country, they go into a long sleep, sometimes coming out during warm periods in late winter. By early spring, the skunk awakens from its torpor and is fully active.

Raccoon

The raccoon inhabits the woodland edge, particularly near salt marshes and the shore. It is known for its black mask, ringed tail, and habit of "washing" food before eating. Actually it only investigates the morsel, turning it over and poking into all corners. Raccoons eat both plants and animals, depending on the season. Young muskrats, squirrels, rabbits, eggs, mussels, clams, and berries are common foods. Loon eggs are particularly vulnerable to raccoon predation, as loons nest in exposed, ground-level areas along freshwater lakes. Raccoons are attracted to lake-side cottages (and nearby garbage cans) with the side effect of damaging the loon population. As for garden raids—there are as many guaranteed methods of safeguarding corn against raccoons as there are raccoons themselves.

The raccoon is not a traveler and lives within a range of one square mile. It forages at night and likes to sun itself on a tree limb during the day. In Maine, raccoons are active all winter. Farther north, they are not true hibernators but can live off stored fat (as much as one inch thick on their backs) during inclement weather. Raccoons have a distinctive family system. Males wander from den to den and may have a number of mates, but females give birth and raise the young without any male assistance.

Raccoon scats are tubes 3/4 inch in diameter with flat ends, quite uniform in consistency. They contain bits of crayfish, insects, shells, and sometimes hair. The tracks are distinctive handlike prints. The animal "paces," moving both left feet forward, then both right feet forward, as contrasted to the opposing gait of most animals. The tracks are usually in pairs, with one hind foot next to one forward foot.

Further Reading and Reference

A Field Guide to Animal Tracks by Olaus J. Murie (Houghton Mifflin Company, 1975)

A Field Guide to the Mammals by William H. Burt and Richard Grossenheider (Houghton Mifflin Company, 1975)

A Guide to Nature in Winter by Donald Stokes (Little, Brown and Company, 1976). Clear, easy to use identification book concerning many aspects of winter ecology.

Marine Life

". . . And as the land is full of God's great blessings, so is the sea replenished with great abundance of excellent fish, of cod sufficient to laden many ships, which we found is upon the coast in the month of June, seals to make oil withal, mullets, turbots, mackerel, herring, crabs, lobsters, oysters and mussels with ragged pearls in them," wrote the English Captain Martin Pring in 1603.

But the current description of Maine's marine resources is hardly the same. The story of nearly all marine organisms which are of value to humans is similar: abundance, heavy catch, relative scarcity. Certainly particular factors related to the animal's life cycle, environmental changes, food supply, disease, etcetera, are linked to the size of the population. But in one example after another—whales, seals, lobster, mackerel, cod—a once flourishing fishery has decreased or ceased altogether.

This section differs somewhat from the other wildlife chapters. Rather than briefly describing a number of species, two animals are considered in depth. Lobsters and whales not only point up some of the more complex issues involved, but they are colorful and intriguing creatures. Summaries of other shellfish, marine mammals, fish, and ocean-going birds are then presented in chart form.

Lobsters

Lobster is top-of-the-line Maine seafood. Boiled lobster, the simplest of dishes, brings the highest price in any restaurant, in-state or out. But such was not always the case. Colonists considered lobsters inferior food and collected them for fertilizer. During the 1800s inmates in state prisons were cut back from three to two days a week of lobster because people thought they might be poisonous. There were others, though, who enjoyed the cheap and abundant resource and eventually the seafood became popular.

The early "fishery" consisted of picking lobsters from between rocks

Lobster.

at low tide. Open-water fishing did not begin until the 1840s, and the familiar wooden traps were brought into use in the 1900s. Lobstering is presently a multi-million dollar business. In 1977 the landed value of lobster in Maine, which reflects only the amount paid to lobstermen, was over 32 million dollars.

Life History

Lobsters mate soon after the mature female molts. Sperm are deposited in a receptacle and stored until the female extrudes her eggs, often up to a year later. The eggs are then fertilized and held in a sticky mass which adheres to the swimmerettes, small legs under the tail. Hence egg-bearing females are termed "berried." Ten to twelve months later the eggs hatch and small, mosquitolike larvae are released. The larvae molt—shed their shell and grow a new, larger shell—several times before they take on the lobster form and descend to the ocean floor. Juveniles and young adults can grow up to 14% in length and 50% in weight after a molt. They molt several times a year until they have reached five inches carapace length, the distance along the back between head and tail. Growth at this point is slower, and annual molting is more usual.

Understanding this life cycle is critical to understanding the present status of the lobster and the industry. It takes seven years for a lobster to achieve legal catch size (3 3/16 inches carapace), but most females are not sexually mature at this time. Since 90% of the Maine catch consists of lobsters which have reached legal size in the previous molt, a large number of sexually immature females are harvested every year. These females never contribute to the pool of larvae or overall lobster population.

Other factors come into play. For example, a sublegal lobster may be caught and released six or seven times, with subsequent handling and increase in mortality, before it reaches legal size. Furthermore, over 300,000 traps are lost annually and each "ghost trap" imprisons two or three lobsters. An estimated one million lobsters perish each year in this way.

Sea temperature also influences abundance of lobster. Warm water stimulates molting, thereby increasing growth and producing a larger crop. 1974-1976 sea temperatures were as warm as the previous peak catch years and there should have been an increase in lobsters. But despite the fact that more traps than ever were set, there was no rise in catch. Instead, the annual haul between 1967 and 1975 dropped 59% and the average size went from nine to two pounds.

Regulations

No one denies that the industry is declining, that "it isn't what it used to be," but few individuals agree about what action should be taken. Maine laws are the strictest along the Northwest Atlantic Coast. Lobsters must be at least 3 3/16 inches and not more than 5 inches carapace length. (The upper limit is based on the controversial hypothesis that larger lobsters bear more eggs and are therefore more valuable as producers. Maine is the only state to enforce an upper limit, and although biologists feel that the law is not necessary, fishermen consistently favor the measure.) Berried females are notched on the tail and returned to the ocean and V-notched females must always be thrown back. In this way, females which do become bearers are protected. A new law requires that traps contain escape vents for sublegal lobsters, to protect young lobsters from over-handling as well as to reducing nonusable catch. This new regulation will also decrease the number of lobsters lost in ghost traps, although it will not entirely solve the problem.

The most controversial proposal concerns an increase in the minimum catch size, gradually changing from 3 3/16 inches to 3 1/2 inches carapace. The increase would allow an additional molt (and 50% weight increase) per lobster and would permit more females to become sexually mature. However, the measure would involve severe financial hardship to fishermen, for even an 1/6-inch increase would mean a drastic reduction in legal catch. A law designed to help the long-term fishery could spell immediate disaster to many lobstermen.

Lobstermen generally favor limiting the overall effort rather than catch size. Limiting licensing, higher license fees, and closing areas by season are all suggestions being considered at the present time.

Whatever the outcome, it is clear that the age-old system of hauling traps by hand is gone forever, and that lobstering is an industry comparable to any other in Maine. Like other industries, supply, demand and price bear heavily on the politics. The decrease in catch has been coupled with an increase in per-pound value. Even though lobster landings dropped ½ million pounds from 1976 to 1977, the value of that landing was up by almost 3 million dollars. Although lobsters are declining, the industry itself carries on.

Commercial Shellfish Found in Maine Waters

Species	Notes on Life, History, Abundance
Lobster	See text
Northern shrimp	Show great fluctuation in population, possibly because Gulf of Maine is lower limit of range and therefore not prime breeding area. Shrimp spawn inshore along mid-coast, producing only males. The young migrate offshore, usually to Jeffrey's Ledge. When three years old, they develop ovaries and migrate inshore to spawn.
Soft-shelled clam	Also known as "long-necked" or "steamers." Feed on microscopic plants filtered from water, hence termed filter feeders. Found in intertidal zone, buried in mud or sand. Very sensitive to environmental factors like pollution and oil spills. 20% of Maine's clam flats are too polluted and closed to harvest, but slightly polluted clams can be purified if placed in a clean environment for period of time. Clams can also accumulate toxin from "Red tide," microscopic plant which is harmless to shellfish but can produce illness and death in humans. Red tide is a problem when the plant grows explosively. All clams in Maine dug by hand with pronged utensil, "hoe." Clamming regulated by local ordinance, requires license.
Sea scallop	Found on sandy bottom but are not burrowers like clams. Can move by opening and closing shell with "adductor" muscle, part of shellfish which is eaten. Harvested by trawling.
Blue mussel	Thin-shelled bivalves attach to intertidal rocks and pilings with byssal threads. Considered gourmet food in Europe but new to American tastes, therefore not widely eaten. Often contain tiny, irregularly shaped pearls.

Quahog	Uncommon bivalves in Maine's cold waters. Some quahog beds located in Casco Bay area between Yarmouth and Phippsburg. Harvesting regulated by local ordinance.
American oyster	Although once abundant along coast, as indicated by Indian shell heaps, now only two areas in state naturally support sizable populations of oyster and these beds are not pollution free. Potential for aquaculture maintains interest in species.

Commercial Fish Found in Maine Waters

Species	Notes on Life, History, Abundance
Herring	Mainstay of fishing industry. Small fish which feed on plankton and smaller fish, in turn fed on by cod, haddock, pollock, hake, whales, and other predaceous fish in the Gulf. Herring used as sardines and kippers, also smoked, dry-salted, and pickled.
Cod	Move inshore in winter and offshore in summer. Inshore cod average 35 pounds, though 200-pound fish have been recorded. Used fresh, frozen, dried; often combined with other fish to make convenience foods, such as fish sticks.
Haddock	Smaller than cod, averaging 1-5 pounds. High value fish, sold fresh and frozen.
Hake	Less important than haddock and cod. Small percentage sold as fillets, remainder used for industrial feeds.
Pollock	Pollock feed on a variety of young fish, grow to 4-15 pounds. Sold frozen and breaded, but not yet wide consumer acceptance.
Whiting	Small fish which feed on all species of young, including their own. Also called "silver hake." New to list of harvested fish in Maine. Abundant in summer months, especially in Casco Bay. Sold frozen or fresh.

Whales

There is no excitement equal to seeing a whale. A blow or a flip of the tail and the creature is gone, but the memory of a behemoth, a giant among animals, remains. Whales have always sparked imagination and awe, from the tale of Jonah to Moby Dick. Although in appearance they

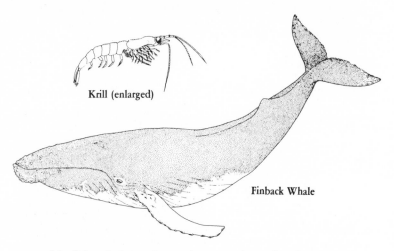

Krill (enlarged)

Finback Whale

resemble fish, whales and porpoises—together referred to as cetaceans—are actually of a much different physical and intellectual order.

It is thought that whales developed from land mammals beginning more than fifty million years ago. Forearms developed into flippers and legs evolved into a tail, leaving two small, vestigal pelvic bones along the "lower" part of the spine. Also, the characteristic fur of all mammals disappeared except for a few patches of hairs in some species. In other ways, whales have preserved the traits of land mammals. They breathe air (rather than obtaining oxygen from water, as fish do), have warm blood, bear their young alive, and suckle the calves.

History

Whales have recently stimulated much public interest. Recordings of "songs" and other sounds indicate that they communicate and have a high level of intelligence. Historical interest, however, has centered on oil and baleen. Whales have an insulating layer of fat, or blubber, which can be rendered into high grade lamp and lubrication oil. Blubber can be up to two feet thick all around the animal in some species,

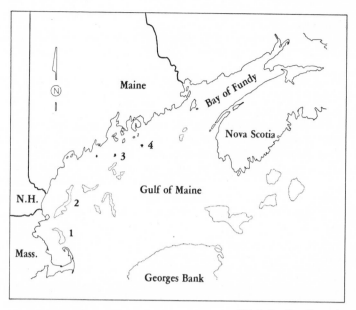

Whale Feeding Grounds
Favorite whale feeding grounds in Gulf of Maine include (1) Stellwagan Bank;
(2) Jeffreys Ledge; (3) Matinicus Rock, and (4) Mount Desert Rock. (Dotted line
indicates 50 fathom mark.)

and hundreds of barrels can be rendered from such a whale. In the hey-
day of the industry, whales fueled the lamps of many coastal towns and
villages. Baleen, or whalebone, was also in high demand for use in um-
brellas, combs, corsets, and scrimshaw.

The right whale, which abounded in Atlantic waters, was the chief
target of whalers in the 1600s and 1700s because it yielded large quantities of oil and baleen and because it floated (as opposed to sinking)
when killed. But by 1750, right whales were nearly exterminated and
American whaling turned to sperm whales. The biggest whaling ports
were located in southern New England—Nantucket, New Bedford,
Martha's Vineyard—rather than in Maine. However, coastal ships from
Winter Harbor, Prospect, Tremont, and other Maine towns did bring in
small numbers of humpbacks and finbacks during the mid-1800s.

Present Status

In 1972 Congress passed the Marine Mammal Protection Act, which prohibits hunting and killing of marine mammals by United States citizens. Most nations have stopped hunting whales—notable exceptions are the Soviet Union and Japan—though not before thousands and thousands of whales were slaughtered and more than one species neared extinction.

Twenty-one species of whales and porpoises have been reported in the Gulf of Maine. Five of these are commonly seen. Most sightings are from cruise vessels, fishing boats or ferries which cross from Maine to Nova Scotia, though whales are also frequently spotted from lighthouses on Campobello Island and West Quoddy Head. Chartered whale and birdwatching trips are sponsored by Allied Whale, a research group at College of the Atlantic in Bar Harbor, as well as various Audubon Socities.

Whales migrate into Cape Cod Bay in early spring and become numerous in the northern portions of the Gulf of Maine in late spring and summer. Favorite feeding areas include Stellwagen Bank, Jeffreys Ledge, Matinicus Rock-Seal Island and Mt. Desert Rock. Groups of diving birds in these areas indicate fish or plankton and may also be a sign of whales feeding nearby. Important field marks include profile and length of whale, shape and color of flukes, and the presence and location of light patches.

Marine Mammals Common to the Gulf of Maine

SPECIES	FIELD MARKS, NOTES ON HABITAT AND BEHAVIOR
Harbor porpoise	Found in inshore waters, often seen in small groups. Smallest of whales, average 5½ feet. Fin triangular with slight concave curve to trailing edge. Usually shy of boats.
Pilot whale (pothead)	Best field marks: coal black color, bulbous kettle-shaped head, and dorsal fin which is much longer at the base than at the top. Seen in groups ranging from 5-100. Average 14 feet long. Feed on squid, small fish, invertebrates.
Finback whale	Most common large whale in Gulf, averages 60 feet. Best field marks: white stripe across right side of jaw; left side of jaw is dark. A light band continues from right jaw to blow-hole and two pale chevrons form a wide V across the back and sides. Eats small

fish and krill (shrimplike crustaceans).

Minke whale	Smallest baleen whale in Gulf, usually 20 feet or less. Broad white stripe across flippers good field mark. Seen alone or in pairs, sometimes very close to ships or shore. Often swims into bays and harbors in pursuit of fish. Usually does not make a visible spout.
Humpback whale	Easily identified by long white flippers; lumpy knobs on head, snout, flippers; acrobatic behavior (often jumps from water); and light/dark patterns on flukes. Each humpback has individual fluke pattern, like large fingerprint, so that photographs of flukes are extremely important. Seen singly, in pairs, or in small groups. Feeds on fish and krill.
Right whale	Historically common, though rarely seen at present. Averages 44 feet in length, has no dorsal fin (all other baleen whales in Gulf do). Spout appears V-shaped when seen from fore or aft.
Harbor seal	Seen on half-tide ledges, small harbor islands, or swimming. Average 5-6 feet length, fur varies from light gray to tan, brown, or black, depending on wetness. Permanent resident. Estimated 6000 or more individuals in Maine. Most often seen in lower Penobscot Bay, near Mt. Desert Island, and in Machias Bay.
Gray seal	Not common but seen occasionally around Mt. Desert Island, Swans Island, and lower Penobscot Bay. Large seal, averaging 7-9 feet. Identified by "Roman nose," large squarish muzzle. Immatures often confused with harbor seals. Coat appears gray when wet (as all seals do) but actually mixed gray, brown, black. Estimated 100 individuals summer in Maine.

Note: Whales and porpoises are divided into two groups, according to methods of feeding. Toothed whales are generally small animals which prey on fish and squid. Baleen whales are larger and have many stiff plates which strain copepods, krill, and other small marine creatures from ocean water. Harbor porpoise and pilot whales are toothed, while finback, minke, humpback, and right whales are rorquals, or baleen whales.

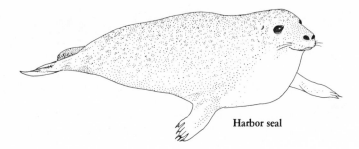

Harbor seal

Pelagic Birds of Maine Waters

SPECIES	NOTES ON ABUNDANCE
Northern fulmar	Common, Oct-Mar
Shearwaters	
Greater shearwater	Common, June-Sept
Sooty shearwater	Uncommon, May-Sept
Petrels	
Leach's storm petrel	Common, May-Sept
Wilson's storm petrel	Common, May-Aug
Gannet	Common, Apr-May, Aug-Oct
Phalaropes	
Red phalarope	Common, Aug-Sept
Northern phalarope	Common, July-Aug
Jaegers and Skuas	
Pomarine jaeger	Common, Aug-Sept
Parasitic jaeger	Common, Aug-Sept
Great skua	Uncommon, June-Sept
Black-legged kittiwake	Common, Oct-Mar
Alcids	
Razorbill	Uncommon, Sept-Mar
Common murre	Uncommon, Sept-Apr
Thick-billed murre	Uncommon, Sept-Mar
Dovekie	Uncommon, Nov-Mar
Black guillemot	Common, all year
Common puffin	Uncommon, Mar-Dec

Further Reading and Reference

The Commercial Fisheries of Maine by Cyrus Hamlin and John R. Ordway (Maine Sea Grant Bulletin 5, available from Ira C. Darling Center)

A Field Guide to the Whales and Seals of the Gulf of Maine by Steve Katona, David Richardson, and Robin Hazard (Printed by Maine Coast Printers, 1975)

Harvesters of the Sea: The Story of Maine's Commercial Fisheries. This booklet and other material is available from the Department of Marine Resources, Augusta, Maine 04333.

Maine Commercial Fisheries, a tabloid newspaper published by Fisheries Communications, Stonington, Maine.

Miscellaneous pamphlets describing the life history of lobster, shrimp, and crabs available from Marine Extension Specialist, Ira C. Darling Center, Walpole, Maine 04573.

Whales in the Gulf of Maine, 1977: Annual Report of the Gulf of Maine Whale Sighting Network by Cathy Ramsdell (College of the Atlantic, 1978)

Forest

When explorers and fishermen sailed to Maine's shores, they saw a forest primeval, "overgrowne for the most part with most sorts of excellent good woods," towering conifers and hardwoods in a nearly untouched forest. The vegetation which covered Maine was the result of uninterrupted evolution from glacial till to climax forest. As the glacier retreated, it left a tundra-like landscape of exposed bedrock, sandy outwash plains, and rocky till. Only arctic plants could grow in the poor substrate and cold climate. As the region warmed and soil accumulated, trees began to move north. Pollen records indicate that the spruce-fir forest did not cover Maine until 2-3000 years ago. Extensive forests now stretch from Maine into a huge belt which sweeps across Canada and circles the Arctic.

The state's "per-humid" climate, a weather system associated with frequent rain, fog, cool summer temperatures and warm winters, allows some tundra plants to remain along the coast. Severe conditions at the beginning of summer, resulting from the chilling influence of the ocean, cause a displaced growing season. Arctic plants like crowberry and cranberry grow in the early summer period, while more temperate plants grow later after ocean temperatures have moderated.

Spruce and fir, mixed with cedar, tamarak, hemlock, maple, birch, and beech now dominate the northern part of Maine. White pine, red pine, and hemlock, in combination with aspen, birch, and maple vegetate much of southern Maine. White pine is the climax species (the tree that will naturally dominate the forest if there is no intervention) in the sandy regions of the state.

History of Maine's Forest

White pine is historically the most important species in the state. Settlers used its straight-grained, durable, plentiful wood for countless projects. Huge trees, the largest with diameters of 6 feet standing 200 feet high, caught the eye of the British Admiralty, who continually searched for mast trees. The King declared that all pines with a 24-inch diameter and larger—regardless of where they grew—were to be marked with the broad arrow and reserved as the King's Pines. Maine colonists, irritated by the law, occasionally defied their sovereign and discretely laid down planks 23 3/4 inches wide lest a government official visit their home.

The first saw mill was set up on the banks of the Salmon Falls River, and many mills followed. Accessible pines along waterways were taken first, but by 1700 loggers ranged 20 miles inland, dragging the trees out with oxen. Demand for barrels for the West Indies trade increased pressure and the ring of axes and crash of falling trees sounded in the forest. Loggers moved upriver and inland. They set up dams, sluices, haul roads, yards and drives. By 1800 the great era of logging had begun. Meanwhile, citizens of coastal towns, like Belfast and Waldoboro, decried the lack of trees and complained of a shortage of firewood.

By 1850 most of the huge pines had been cut. Timbermen turned to spruce during the last half of the century. Meanwhile, a small pulp wood factory in Norway, Maine, laid the foundation for a third wave of timber cutting, this time for paper-making. Because the paper industry demanded constant and continuing fiber, the "cut out and get out" philosophy of the previous generation was replaced with forest management techniques aimed at stabilizing the timber stands.

Today, spruce and fir cover 90% of Washington and Hancock Counties. Over half of the land is owned by St. Regis Pejepscot, and Georgia Pacific Paper companies. Further south white pine and mixed hardwoods predominate and 70-80% of the land is wooded, although most is privately owned.

White Pine Succession

Succession is the orderly replacement of one plant community with another community as sunlight, water, and soil nutrient conditions change. When "Ohio fever" infected farmers in the early 1800s, they left their land for richer soil in the Midwest and a unique situation resulted. The abandoned fields were open to growth, but only one species—white pine—was both sunlight-tolerant and had seeds heavy enough to work down through the grass cover. Oaks and beech, which have heavy seeds, need the protection of shade as seedlings. Birch and aspen, which grow well in sunny areas, have light-weight seeds which cannot move past the grass cover and into the soil. By the 1900s, thick pine stands occupied land where corn and other crops once grew. Stone

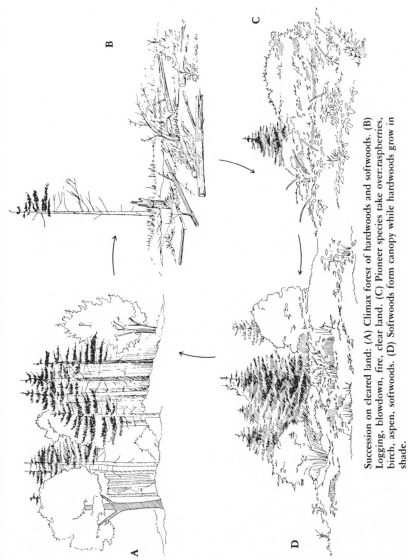

Succession on cleared land: (A) Climax forest of hardwoods and softwoods. (B) Logging, blowdown, fire, clear land. (C) Pioneer species take over: raspberries, birch, aspen, softwoods. (D) Softwoods form canopy while hardwoods grow in shade.

walls which separated fields were enveloped in a forest. Nearly all white pine stands were once farmland, and even the well known Bowdoin Pines in Brunswick are second-growth pine in an old field. Unless the stand is located on a sandy plain where pine is the climax species, succession will continue, and hardwoods will invade the area.

Forest Succession

Succession also takes place in the forest itself. When fire, blowdown or logging create an open area, raspberries, aspen, white birch, and conifers pioneer the region. Hardwood seedlings root in the shade of these sun-loving species. Later, when the conifers become over-mature or if they fall from wind or disease, hardwood saplings take over. Most often a mixed stand of hardwoods and softwoods of varying ages will populate a forest.

Natural disasters (such as the spruce budworm epidemic which has decimated Maine's northern timberlands) and man-made disasters (like the great fire on Mount Desert which destroyed 17,000 acres of spruce and pine) serve to clear the land and initiate the sequence of succession on a large scale.

In a sense, timber management practices resemble processes which occur naturally. Selective cutting takes individual trees, leaving "windows" of light and space similar to those which occur when individual trees die or are blown over. Clear-cutting eliminates all or nearly all trees in a given area and produces an even-aged stand, much like an epidemic or fire. Of course, the analogy is limited, for a variety of other factors—economic, political, social—intervene in timber stand management.

Parts of a Forest

Most mention has been made of the dominant species which, in the climax stage, would form the canopy, or top layer of vegetation. Many other plants live in the forest community, depending on the availability of light, water, and nutrients. Striped maple, mountain maple, mountain ash, witch-hazel, and many species of viburnum are smaller trees and shrubs which form the understory. Where the soil is relatively rich, plants such as clintonia, wood sorrel, starflower, goldthread, bunchberry, twinflower, and lady slipper—beautiful flowering plants of the north woods—can be found. In dense forest with poor soil, mosses, ferns, and decomposers like Indian pipe are common.

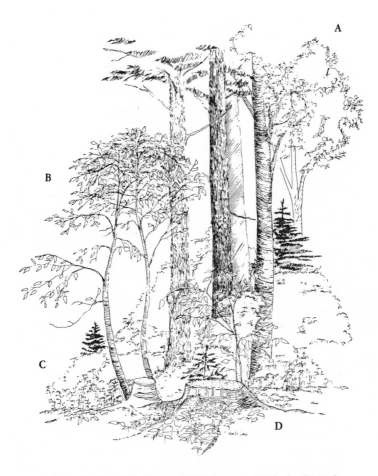

Parts of a forest: (A) Canopy (B) Understory (C) Shrub (D) Herb

Birds of the Forest

At any one spot in the forest, a birdwatcher can survey many habitats, from low-lying brush to lofty treetops. An eye trained to watch all levels of the woods, plus a familiarity with which birds frequent which type of woods, provides an exciting walk and a bird list which can range from towhees to hawks.

SPECIES	Mixed Woods	Coniferous Woods	Deciduous Woods	Notes
Hawks				
Sharp-shinned	X			Common, migrant
Cooper's	X			Uncommon, migrant
Red-tailed	X			Common, migrant
Red-shouldered	X			Uncommon, migrant
Broad-winged	X			Common, summer
Grouse				
Ruffed	X			Common, resident
Spruce		X		Uncommon, resident
Black-Billed Cuckoo	X			Common, summer
Owls				
Great Horned	X			Uncommon, resident
Barred	X	X		Uncommon, resident
Long-eared	X			Uncommon, Mar-Nov
Saw-whet	X	X		Uncommon, resident
Whip-Poor-Will	X			Common, summer
Woodpeckers				
Common Flicker	X			Common, summer
Pileated woodpecker	X			Uncommon, resident
Yellow-bellied sapsucker	X		X	Common, summer
Hairy woodpecker	X		X	Common, resident
Downy woodpecker	X			Common, resident
Black-backed three-toed woodpecker	X	X		Uncommon, resident
Flycatchers				
Yellow-bellied flycatcher		X		Common, summer
Least flycatcher			X	Common, summer
Eastern wood pewee			X	Common, summer
Olive-sided flycatcher		X		Uncommon, summer
Jays and Crows				
Gray jay		X		Uncommon, resident
Blue jay	X			Common, resident
Common raven	X			Common, resident
Common crow	X			Common, resident

SPECIES	Mixed Woods	Coniferous Woods	Deciduous Woods	Notes
Chickadees				
Black-capped	X			Common, resident
Boreal		X		Common, resident
Nuthatches				
White-breasted nuthatch	X			Common, resident
Red-breasted nuthatch		X		Common, resident
Brown creeper	X	X		Common, resident
Winter Wren		X		Common, summer
Thrushes				
Wood			X	Common, summer
Hermit	X			Common, summer
Swainson's	X	X		Common, summer
Veery			X	Common, summer
Kinglets				
Golden-crowned		X		Common, summer
Ruby-crowned	X	X		Common, summer
Vireos				
Solitary	X	X		Common, summer
Red-eyed	X			Common, summer
Warblers				
Black-and-white warbler			X	Common, summer
Tennessee warbler		X		Common, summer
Nashville warbler	X			Common, summer
Parula warbler		X		Common, summer
Magnolia warbler	X			Common, summer
Cape May warbler		X		Common, summer
Black-throated blue warbler	X			Common, summer
Yellow-rumped warbler	X	X		Common, summer
Black-throated green warbler		X		Common, summer
Blackburnian warbler		X		Common, summer
Chestnut-sided warbler	X			Common, summer
Bay-breasted warbler		X		Common, summer
Blackpoll warbler		X		Common, May & Sept
Pine warbler		X		Common, summer
Ovenbird	X			Common, summer
Canada warbler	X			Common, summer
American redstart	X			Common, summer
Scarlet Tanager			X	Common, summer
Grosbeaks, Finches, Sparrows, Buntings				
Rose-breasted grosbeak			X	Common, summer

SPECIES	Mixed Woods	Coni-ferous Woods	Deci-duous Woods	Notes
Indigo bunting			X	Common, summer
Evening grosbeak		X		Common, resident
Purple finch		X		Common, summer
Pine grosbeak		X		Uncommon, resident
Pine siskin	X	X		Uncommon, resident
American goldfinch	X			Common, summer
Red crossbill		X		Uncommon, resident
White-winged crossbill		X		Uncommon, resident
Rufous-sided towhee	X			Common, summer
Dark-eyed junco		X		Common, summer
White-throated sparrow		X		Common, summer

Mammals of Forest and Field

Most people see few of the mammals which inhabit the forest and field. Tiny shrews hide in leaf litter, bats flash by as shadows in the dusk, bobcats prefer territory remote from human habitation. But simply getting familiar with an area—the floor of mixed woods, rocky caves, thick new growth, open field—provides a better chance of seeing animals and their signs. It also develops a fuller sense of the ecosystem itself.

ANIMAL	Notes on habitat or locale. Unless otherwise indicated, range extends all along coast.
Shrews	
Masked shrew	Moist, heavily vegetated woods or brushland
Smoky shrew	Leaf mold layer in birch and hemlock forests
Pygmy shrew	Wet or dry wooded and open areas
Shorttail shrew	Forest floor
Hairytail mole	Upland habitat with good vegetative cover
Bats	
Keen myotis	Forested areas, hollow trees, caves
Little brown myotis	Hollow trees, caves, rock ledges
Small-footed myotis	Forested areas, caves; in southern half of Maine

Red bat	Wooded areas, normally roosts in trees
Big brown bat	Wooded areas, hollow trees, caves
Hoary bat	Wooded areas
Black bear	Remote forested areas (for example, Moosehorn Wildlife Preserve)
Raccoon	Wooded area near streams and lake borders
Weasels	
Fisher	Extensive mixed hardwood forests and cut-over wilderness areas along northern part of coast
Shorttail weasel (ermine)	Prefers coniferous forests but not far from water
Longtail weasel	All land habitats near water but prefers open sites
Striped skunk	Mixed woods, brushland, semi-open country usually within two miles of water and often close to human habitation
Canines	
Eastern coyote	Hemlock-hardwood forests in southern Maine
Red fox	Mixture of forest and open country, especially farmland, meadows, and clearings
Gray fox	Open forests and brushland in southern Maine
Bobcat	Remote forests
Rodents	
Woodchuck (marmot or ground hog)	Prefers open woods, old fields, pastures
Eastern chipmunk	Deciduous forests, brushy areas; not in deep forest
Eastern gray squirrel	Hardwood forests
Red squirrel	Pine and spruce forest or mixed hardwoods
Northern flying squirrel	Coniferous and mixed forests
Mice, rats, voles	
White-footed mouse	Wooded or brushy areas in southern counties only
Deer mouse	Woods near fields, dry-land habitat
Boreal redback vole	Fields, mossy floors of woodlands
Meadow vole	Habitat not restricted
Jumping Mice	
Meadow jumping mouse	Low meadows
Woodland jumping mouse	Heavily wooded habitat

Porcupine	Most types of wooded habitats
Hares and rabbits	
Snowshoe hare	Any type of wooded area, especially second growth forest
New England cottontail	Open forests and brushy areas in southern Maine
Deer	
White-tailed deer	Forests and open brushy areas
Moose	Forests near lakes or swamps in northern two thirds of coast

Further Reading and Reference

Flower Finder by May Theilgaard Watts (Nature Study Guild, 1955). Pocket-sized booklet, pictorial key very easy to use.

A Guide to New England's Landscape by Neil Jorgensen (Barre Publishers, 1971). Chapters about New England forest types, includes places to visit.

Master Tree Finder by May Theilgaard Watts (Nature Study Guild, 1963). Similar to above. Excellent.

Mountain Flowers of New England (Appalachian Mountain Club, 1964). Identification guide to mountain and woodland flora, not just flowers.

Spring Wildflowers of New England by Marilyn Dwelley (Downeast Enterprise Inc., 1973). Identification by color.

Trees and Shrubs of Northern New England by Frederic Steele and Albion Hodgon (Society for the Protection of New Hampshire Forests, 1975). Good identification book.

Rocky Shore

The ocean is storm-tossed and rugged. Huge waves swell in from the horizon, cresting in a swirl of white foam and gray water. The thunder of wave against rock is followed by a long hiss of foam, racing through channels and over boulders, reaching with eager fingers into every hole and crevice, then retreating in miniature cascades and waterfalls. Eider float placidly beyond the cresting waves, while a few guillemots dive for fish. Two large gray seals, distinguished by a massive "Roman nose," loll along the surface 200 yards offshore.

The scene is Mount Desert Island in October (with the exception of the gray seals), but it could be any rocky shore or inlet. The meeting of ocean and land has always been a place of power and awe, especially in regions which stand exposed to the full fury of ocean storms. How many poems, stories, and songs recount the experiences of storm-tossed sailors who survived—or did not survive—the perils of rocky reefs and unmarked shore?

Maine has more than its share of both rocks and coastline. Over 3000 miles of shore are squeezed into the 230 air miles which separate Kittery from Lubec. "This coast is mountainous" with "isles of huge rocks" wrote Captain John Smith in 1614, and the landscape has changed little since then. A look at the map shows that the peninsulas and islands form numerous north-south parallels. These parallels correspond to the folds in rocks which were created when continental plates collided 350 million years ago. Erosion of weaker rock, particularly during glacial times, left the resistant rock in ridges which run from north to south.

Although thousands of feet of rock have been weathered from the surface, Maine has a "youthful" coast characterized by headlands and islands not yet evened out or truncated. This somewhat puzzling circumstance is accounted for by the still-rising ocean, which now covers the older, more eroded areas. As the water level rises, it attacks new headlands and so does not have a chance to "age" an area for view.

The plants and animals of the rocky shore live in a peculiar habitat strictly governed by the tide. Tides are the unceasing movement of water, caused by the gravitational pull of the moon and, to a smaller degree, the sun and planets. In Maine, two high tides and two low tides form one tidal day of 24 hours 50 minutes, reflecting the length of a lunar day. Just as the moon rises 50 minutes later each night, so the tide comes in 50 minutes later from one day to the next.

Average tide heights depend on the area. Portland has a 9-foot tide, Eastport 20, while the Bay of Fundy—which is famous for its changing water level—boasts a 50-foot tide. Each month, two particularly high tides occur when the moon, sun, and earth line up and the gravitational pull is strongest. These "spring tides" occur during full moon and new moon and have no relation to the season. Especially low tides occur when the sun and moon are at right angles to the earth, and pull is counterbalanced. Neap tides as they are called, occur twice monthly when the moon is quartered. It follows that there is no single high-water or low-water mark, but that the level fluctuates slightly throughout the monthly cycle.

Zonation

Tides create zones on the rocky shore. Plants and animals are distributed in horizontal bands ranging from sub-tidal through supra-tidal habitat. The species arrange themselves according to the extent of water, air, sun and wind exposure they can tolerate. Zonation may best be observed at low tide on a steep slope, but it also occurs in the salt marsh and sandy beach. Quite different environmental conditions in each zone require particular adaptations and allow a variety of species to live in proximity.

Laminarian Zone

Kelps live at and below the low tide level in the Laminarian Zone. These large, leathery brown seaweeds—actually brown algae—may weigh 25 pounds each. Kelps survive the pounding waves by strength, flexibility and secure foothold. One species of seaweed can withstand 600 pounds per square inch before breaking, but normally the blades wash back and forth with the waves to avert the brutal force. Kelps attach to rocks by means of a holdfast, a mass of root-like tentacles. In a storm, the rock will often dislodge before the holdfast is broken; kelps washed ashore usually still cling to their rock base.

The Laminarian Zone most closely resembles the ocean environment. Vegetation is always inundated, and the kelps may live at some depth.

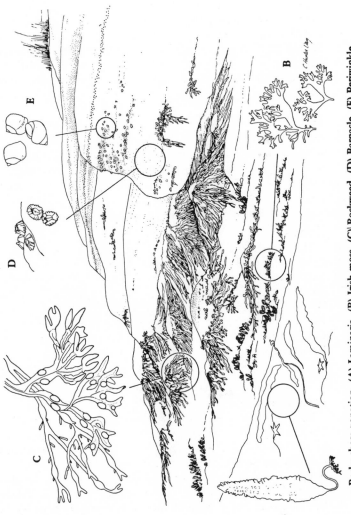

Rocky shore zonation. (A) Laminaria (B) Irish moss (C) Rockweed (D) Barnacle (E) Periwinkle

Scientists speculate that laminarias developed millions of years ago when the earth was layered with clouds. The kelps developed the ability to photosynthesize with filtered rather than direct sunlight, so they were also able to live in an underwater environment.

Crabs, sea urchins, starfish, anemones, sponges, marine worms and jellyfish inhabit the Kelp Zone. The starfish is a particularly fascinating creature. To obtain food, the animal can wrap its arms around the tightly closed shell of a mussel or clam. Its superior strength forces the shell open. The starfish then pushes its stomach out through its mouth and into the shell, digesting the bivalve "on site."

Irish Moss Zone

Above the kelps lies the Irish Moss Zone, dominated of course by Irish moss. This red seaweed, which is also an algae, grows into a shrubby, much-branched plant several inches high. Carrageenan, a colloid used as a stabilizer and thickener in toothpaste, paint, chocolate milk, ice cream and other products, is manufactured from this seaweed. Irish moss is also the key ingredient in blancmange, a traditional Irish moss pudding made by cooking young seaweed, milk and flavoring.

Irish moss and its associates—dulse, laver and sea lettuce—live below average low tide but are exposed twice a month during neap tides. Crabs, sea urchins, starfish and mussels take cover in the seaweeds, retreating to the Laminarian Zone during the lowest tides.

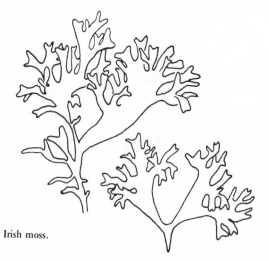

Irish moss.

Rockweed Zone

Bladder wrack and knotted wrack seaweeds dominate the intertidal, or Rockweed Zone. A close inspection of bladder wrack reveals small air sacs which enable the plant to float near the surface when the tide is in. Rockweeds are brown algae like kelps and attach to the rock by means of a holdfast. This seaweed is often used to pack lobsters for shipment.

Periwinkles, dog welks and limpets use rockweed for protection from the drying effects of wind and sun, for even on a hot day the seaweed is damp beneath its outer layer. Periwinkles are mobile snails with shells. As they move along, they scrape bits of food from seaweed with a sand-papery tongue, called a radulla. A large periwinkle population can severely damage or even wipe out a seaweed stand. Periwinkles live all over the world and in several zones on the rock slope. Darker shelled animals live lower in the water, lighter shelled animals live nearer the surface. Each periwinkle has adapted to living in its particular zone and could not swap places with its relative.

Dog welks resemble periwinkles but are carnivorous. They use their radulla to bore through shells of mussels, barnacles, and dead crabs. A. clam shell with a tiny circular hole near its apex tells a tale of dog welk predation.

Barnacle Zone

Barnacles form a white layer which marks the high tide. Young, free-swimming shrimplike animals cement themselves to a rock, boat, or piling, secreting a six-plated shell. The Barnacle Zone takes the most abuse from waves. Although a barnacle can be easily crushed by the direct blow of a hammer, the dome-shaped shell can withstand a wave force of up to 40 pounds per square inch. Water cannot crash directly against a barnacle, but slides off the shell and the energy is dissipated. During low tide, barnacles close their shells and wait; during high tide, they open up and strain minute food particles from the water with thin, feathery legs.

Periwinkle Zone

The rough periwinkle lives on the boundary between land and water. Only spring tides reach the Periwinkle Zone. The animal must maintain some contact with salt water, but it has characteristics of land snails. For example, females produce live young instead of laying eggs. These periwinkles live on blue-green algae and seek the protection of damp, cool crevices in the rock.

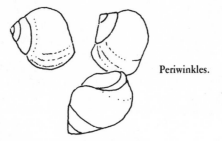

Periwinkles.

Black Zone

Immediately above the Periwinkle Zone lies a layer of black, tarlike material. Black lichen (*Verrucaria*) and blue-green algae (*Calothrix*) subsist on the deserted rock. They are regularly splashed, but are not covered by the tide. Few animals except periwinkles venture into the Black Zone.

Above the Zones

A band of bare rock usually separates the life of the shore from the forest edge. Plants which grow near the ocean are exposed to salt spray during storms (one cup of salt in each gallon of water) and constantly struggle against wind pruning and dehydration. Fewer varieties grow on the coast than inland, and often the plants are dwarfed or misshapen. Black spruce, pine, juniper, bayberry, lowbush blueberry, bunchberry, and a crusty orange lichen called *Zanthoria* are often found along the shore.

Tide Pools

Rocky crevices and basins which lie in the intertidal zone trap water and support a special community of flora and fauna, a microcosm of shoreline life. The inhabitants can adapt to a changing salt concentration, for evaporation makes the content higher and rains dilute the pools. Also, the temperature range is great and may change quickly. Inhabitants from much lower zones, like starfish, limpets, sea anemones and sea lettuce, are found in tide pools. Some species of seaweeds have hollow tubes which trap oxygen produced during photosynthesis and, on a sunny day, the gas will slowly escape and bubble to the surface. The best way to observe a tide pool is to sit quietly by the side, face near the water. After the creatures have recovered from their fright, they will resume their normal activities.

Wildlife

Although no birds or mammals nest in the intertidal zone, a number of each group may be seen nearby. White-tailed deer, raccoon, squirrel, porcupines, skunk, and other forest animals inhabit the land near the ocean's edge. Harbor seals are often seen sunning on pull-out ledges at low tides, and occasionally gray seals venture near shore. Loons, cormorants and gulls are standard features of offshore waters. Common sightings include:

Loons	
Common	Common, winter
Red-throated	Uncommon, migrant
Cormorants	
Great	Common, winter
Double-crested	Common, summer
Waterfowl	
Greater scaup	Common, winter
Common goldeneye	Common, winter
Barrow's goldeneye	Uncommon, winter
Bufflehead	Common, winter
Oldsquaw	Common, winter
Harlequin duck	Uncommon, winter
Common eider	Common resident
King eider	Uncommon, winter
White-winged scoter	Common, winter
Surf scoter	Common, winter
Black scoter	Common, winter
Common merganser	Common, resident
Red-breasted merganser	Common, winter
Gulls	
Great black-backed	Common, resident
Herring	Common, resident
Ring-billed	Common, Sept. and Oct.
Laughing	Uncommon, summer
Bonaparte's	Common, May, July-Sept.
Terns	
Common	Common, summer
Arctic	Common, summer
Roseate	Uncommon, summer
Black guillemot	Common, resident

Common eider is a significant species in Maine because it is the state's only breeding sea duck and because Maine is the major nesting site on the Atlantic coast of the United States. Eider breed on more than 200 of Maine's coastal islands, primarily from Pemaquid Point to Schoodic Peninsula. Although the eider population was devastated in the late 1800s and early 1900s by egg and plumage hunters, the birds have since made a comeback, and a number of nesting islands are now protected.

Beacons of the Shore

If the rocky coast typifies Maine, lighthouses typify the rocky coast. For almost 200 years, keepers have attended lighthouses in Maine. The job was a solitary outpost on the frontier, a crucial link in maritime safety. Seventy-seven lighthouses mark dangerous ledges and headlands from Isles of Shoals to West Quoddy Head. Each structure has its own history and personality, and they weave together into a fabric of colorful character. One keeper waved farewell to his wife, rowed toward the nearest port for supplies, and was never seen again. Another keeper had trouble maintaining his light because huge masses of monarch butterflies smothered the flame. A third keeper's wife tied her children to a line so they would not wander within reach of the waves. Tradition bound any boat visiting the lighthouse on Mt. Desert Rock to bring a box of soil for the tiny flower garden, a garden which was washed away each winter by storms.

But lighthouses, like everything else, are susceptible to change. In 1939 the U.S. Lighthouse Service was taken over by the U.S. Coast Guard. Today, only 22 of Maine's beacons are still tended. The other 55 are fitted out with automatic fog sensors and light controls. Whoever would be a lighthouse keeper must hurry, for the job may not long be listed in Maine's employment book.

Further Reading and Reference

The Edge of the Sea by Rachael Carson (Houghton Mifflin Company, 1955). Classic text about the coastal environment. Parts were written in New Harbor, Maine.

The Northeast Coast by Maitland Edey (Time, Inc., 1972). A Time-Life series book giving an overall view of the rocky coast; beautiful color pictures.

The Rocky Shore by John M. Kingsbury (The Chatham Press, Inc., 1970). A good identification guide.

Salt Marsh

The Atlantic seaboard is fringed with a ribbon of lush, green marshes, a meeting place between land and ocean. The southern states are most blessed. South Carolina has over 500,000 acres of salt marsh, Virginia almost 200,000, as compared to Maine's scanty 15,500 acres. The glacier is again responsible. When it covered Maine, it reached over the present day mainland and deposited its sediments on Georges Bank. The relative scarcity of soil and the slow erosion of rock to produce new sediments means that Maine is poor in the material that forms the foundation of mud flats and marshes, tiny particles of clay and silt. Even the fine sediments brought downstream by rivers flow out into the Gulf of Maine rather than being trapped by sand bars or deltas.

Salt Marsh Formation

In some areas—shallow, protected inlets where waves wash sediments toward shore—the marsh is able to get a start. Suspended particles sink when they reach slack water and adhere to the bottom. Layer upon layer accumulates, held in place by natural cohesion and a cover of eelgrass. Mudflats are formed when the particles are submerged at high tide but are exposed at low tide.

Seeds of the *Spartina* grass are blown onto the mud, or a mat of grass is washed ashore from some eroded marsh nearby. The *Spartina* is specially adapted to the rigorous salt water regime and quickly establishes itself by sending out underground rhizomes or stems. Substrate is provided by the grass itself for as it dies it forms a thick, spongy peat. Particles continue to accumulate between stems and in the peat until the mud flats are built up to the average high tide level. Maine boasts few extensive marshes. The 3,000 acre Scarborough Marsh is the only major area in the state. Instead, the coast is dotted with mudflats and small marsh areas, interludes to the rocky shore and examples of a raw coastline being tamed.

Limiting Factors

The salt marsh poses a challenge to plants and animals alike. Whatever inhabits the marsh must withstand a twice-daily dunking and a large variation in temperature—a hot August afternoon bask will quickly turn into a cold bath when the tide rises. The roots of plants are continually in contact with salt water. Salinity is not constant, though, as rain and creeks bring fresh water to dilute the sea salt. Inhabitants are exposed to searing rays of the sun, pounding storm waves, and the cold fingers of winter ice.

These conditions would kill most living things. But over the years *Spartina* has evolved certain characteristics which enable it to thrive. A particular chemical apparatus keeps out large quantities of harmful salt; what salt is absorbed is collected and excreted by unique glands on the leaves. Thin tubes run from the leaves to the roots to provide oxygen which is not available in the mud. (Bacteria and higher organisms living on the mud surface use all the dissolved oxygen brought in by the tide, leaving sub-surface mud devoid of oxygen. Anerobic or oxygen-less bacteria take over the task of decaying buried organic matter. Hydrogen sulfide is a by-product of this process and contributes the distinctive "rotten egg" smell of marshes.)

Although *Spartina* will grow in fresh water, it is out-competed by plants which are better adapted for those conditions. Instead, it grows in the salt marsh, where no other plant is as well prepared to deal with the harsh demands. As in any system with severe limiting factors, there are few species, but those species are prolific. *Spartina* colonizes the marsh, providing protection for other plants and animals which follow.

Zonation of the Marsh

The flora and fauna which join *Spartina* are shown next page. Each has a particular position, based on its ability to withstand salt and inundation, and the marsh can be divided into broad zones.

Seaweeds and algae live on mud flats and spend half of their lives under water. The tall *Spartina* grass (*Spartina alterniflora*, or salt marsh cord grass) dominates the intertidal zone. Milkwort, a tiny plant with rosy flowers, and glasswort, which seems to have no leaves but only a succulent, branched stem, grow between *Spartina* stems.

The upper marsh, where salt water reaches only twice a month during spring tides, shows a greater diversity. Short *Spartina* (*Spartina patens*, or salt meadow cord grass) grows in swirls and "cowlicks." Sea lavender blooms in the fall, along with the easily recognized seaside goldenrod.

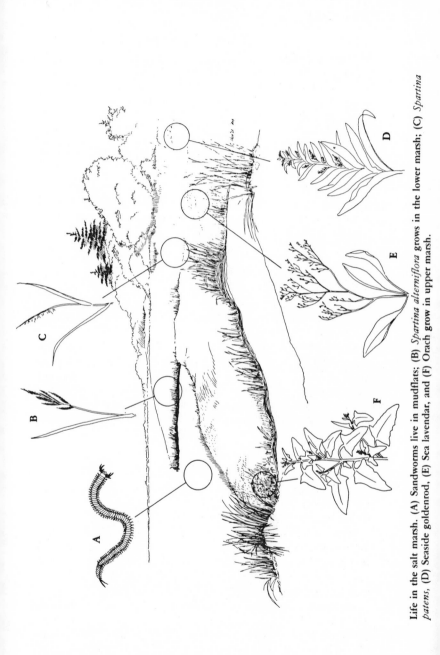

Life in the salt marsh. (A) Sandworms live in mudflats; (B) *Spartina alterniflora* grows in the lower marsh; (C) *Spartina patens*, (D) Seaside goldenrod, (E) Sea lavendar, and (F) Orach grow in upper marsh.

Glasswort also grows here, particularly in salt pans—small depressions in the marsh which trap water during the highest tides. Subsequent evaporation increases salinity, killing all but the most salt-tolerant plants. Glasswort, seaside orach, and seaside plantain are all edible and naturally salted.

Rushes reach from the intertidal zone into the upper shore. Plants which can tolerate salt spray, but not actual flooding, line the marsh and separate it from the forest beyond. Unfortunately, poison ivy thrives in this habitat and poses a hazard to anyone bent on exploration.

Marsh Animals

Few animals make their homes in the marsh. Many live on land or in the air and frequent the marsh at their choosing. Others live in the water, entering with the tide. Immobile organisms have developed adaptations to exposure and salinity problems. The ribbed mussel closes its shell until the tide returns with oxygen and food. Sandworms burrow in the mud. Turtles have a watertight skin. The marsh grasshopper climbs *Spartina* to wait out high tide. If rain dilutes the salt water, soft shell clams can close up and live for as long as a week on stored glycogen until salinity returns to a normal level.

Visitors from the ocean include many varieties of fish which spawn in the marsh or use it as a nursery for their young. Except for mummichugs and killifish which live in tide pools and pans, fish are hard to spot and identify. Mammals are usually active at night and are equally hard to see. Tracks of raccoon, mink, Eastern gray squirrel, deer mouse, meadow vole, muskrat, Norway rat, black rat, and white-tailed deer are found in and about the salt marsh.

Birds of the Marsh

Birds frequent marshes by day and by night for nesting, feeding, and protection. During spring and fall migrations, great numbers of ducks, geese and shorebirds can be seen in the salt marsh and on adjacent mudflats.

SPECIES	Salt Marsh	Mud- flats	Notes
Herons and Allies			
Great blue heron	X	X	Common, April-Oct
Green heron		X	Common, summer
Little blue heron		X	Uncommon, summer

Species	Salt Marsh	Mud-Flats	Notes
Common egret	X	X	Uncommon, summer
Snowy egret	X	X	Common, summer
Louisiana heron	X	X	Uncommon, summer
Black-crowned night heron	X	X	Uncommon, summer
Least bittern	X		Uncommon, summer
American bittern	X	X	Common, summer
Glossy ibis	X		Common, summer
Geese			
Canada goose	X		Common, migrant
Snow goose	X		Common, spring
Waterfowl			
Black duck	X		Common, resident
Pintail	X		Common, migrant
Green-winged teal	X		Common, summer
Blue-winged teal	X		Common, summer
Sora	X		Common, summer
Shorebirds			
Semipalmated plover		X	Common, May, Aug-Sept
Piping plover		X	Uncommon, summer
Black-bellied plover		X	Common, May, Aug-Nov
Ruddy turnstone		X	Common, May, Aug-Oct
Spotted sandpiper		X	Common, summer
Willet	X	X	Uncommon, summer
Greater yellowlegs	X	X	Common, May, Aug-Oct
Lesser yellowlegs	X	X	Common, Aug
Purple sandpiper		X	Common, winter
Pectoral sandpiper	X	X	Common, Sept
Least sandpiper		X	Common, May, Aug-Sept
Dunlin		X	Common, Sept-Oct
Short-billed dowitcher		X	Common, May, July-Sept
Semipalmated sandpiper		X	Common, May, July-Sept
Sanderling		X	Common, July-Sept
Snowy Owl	X		Uncommon, winter
Sharp-tailed sparrow	X		Uncommon, winter

Great blue heron.

Relationship to Man

The salt marsh is one of the most productive environments in the world. It can grow 5-10 tons of organic matter per acre per year. For comparison, good agricultural land yields 1½-5 tons per acre. Organic material unconsumed in the marsh becomes detritus, which is removed by the tide and supports fish life in bays and the ocean. Two thirds of the commercial catch of the East Coast spends some part of its life in the salt marsh. Recognizing the importance of marshes to the fisheries industry, Maine law requires a permit to alter coastal wetland, either private or public.

Early settlers went to the marsh for hay, thatch, fodder and alewives. Maine was known then for its saltwater farms which lined the southern coast. But current demands are much different. Despite the need for preservation, pressure is strong for development. One half of Connecticut's marshland has been filled. Highways which run along the coast of New Jersey bisect what once was productive marsh and is now an industrial blight. In the 1960s Maine lost 1% of its marshland every year—a small amount, but the state has few salt marshes to spare. As Maine continues to grow, especially in the south where most marshes are located, the conflict between expansion and preservation will be even more evident.

The salt marsh is a unique area to investigate by foot or by canoe. Old clothes, well tied tennis shoes or work boots, a sun hat, and mosquito repellent are necessities. Marshes should not be explored alone, as "honey pots" (sink holes of rotten peat) and eroded banks can give way, and more than one explorer has become mired in the gluey mud.

Further Reading and Reference

Life and Death of the Salt Marsh by John and Mildred Teal (Ballentine Books, 1969). The classic book about salt marsh formation and natural history.

Life in and Around the Salt Marshes by Michael Ursin (Thomas Y. Crowell Company, 1972). Excellent introduction to salt marsh and identification of common plants and animals.

Sand Beach

Sandpipers scurry along the water's edge. Dunes stand in a high ridge overlooking the ocean. Waves topple against the smooth sand in an unending procession, playing tag with uncounted numbers of bare feet. The burning August sun is offset by a cool breeze. Sunburn, sandy shoes, squinted eyes—signs of a day at the beach. Long Beach, Crescent Beach, Ogunquit, Moody, Wells, Kennebunk, Goose Rocks, Fortunes Rocks, Old Orchard, Popham, and Reid are all favorite recreational areas. Maine has few beaches compared to southern states, and each swath of sand is treasured.

The Rocky Shore and Beaches

Maine's few beaches are the direct result of three events. First, glaciers deposited large amounts of sand across the state and on the Continental Shelf, which was then above sea level. Second, waves winnowed the sediments, separating them into larger and finer grains, carrying them from one place to another. Third, Maine's coast has numerous rocky fingers. Sediments deposited between headlands were protected and trapped. In a sense, all Maine beaches are "pocket" beaches which formed between promontories, although in some cases the headlands are some distance apart. (The term "pocket beach" more usually refers to small beaches tucked between two proximal fingers of bedrock.)

The rocky shore accounts for major differences between northern beaches and those of the mid-Atlantic states. Sand is contained and protected. There is therefore no large-scale drifting or littoral movement of sand which occurs when waves strike an exposed shore at an angle. Longshore currents (currents which run parallel to the shore) and drift account for massive sand movement on the large, barrier island beaches in North and South Carolina, Virginia and Delaware, but are less important factors in Maine.

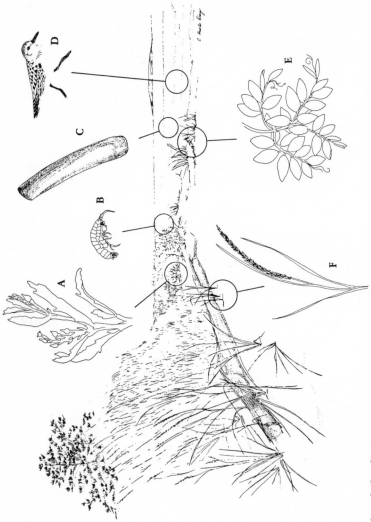

Life at the beach. (A) Sea rocket (B) Sand flea (C) Razor clam (D) Sanderling (E) Beach pea (F) American beachgrass

Change and Equilibrium

After the glaciers receded, after sediments were reworked and deposited in rocky inlets, an equilibrium was reached. The volume of sand in each beach stabilized. Cyclic and small scale changes still occur. Each summer and early fall the beach face is built up, and each winter that sand is moved into the offshore region. But sand movement is chiefly onshore-offshore, rather than from one beach to another. Possibly in the Old Orchard and Popham beach systems located at the mouths of the Saco and Kennebec Rivers—the two rivers which transport glacial sediments downstream—there is a steady resupply of sand, but even that supply is dwindling.

Balance is the key word in understanding Maine's beaches. Each area is influenced by waves, tides, currents, wind and sea level changes. To the casual observer, each beach seems to change dramatically from season to season, from year to year. Waves erode the beach face. Bars build up, migrate, then merge with the mainland. An area of beach grass may disappear under a burden of storm-deposited sand. But each event is part of a cycle. Balance does not mean inertia. With each change comes an adjustment, a new equilibrium.

An influential yet scarcely perceptible phenomenon which affects beaches is sea level rise. Melting of the polar ice cap constantly adds water to the world's oceans, an average of two inches per century over the last 7000 years. As a result, shoreline retreat is more common than rare. Beaches must move inland and upland to keep pace with the ocean. Changes in beach position are inevitable and natural. Problems arise only when change means economic loss. When a beach retreats through a seashore development, for example, natural forces are termed destructive.

Wave Development and Beach Position

Waves exert the major influence on beaches in Maine, although they may form hundreds of miles offshore. Wind creates friction as it passes against the ocean, transferring energy from air to water. "Seas," the irregular waves which move in a variety of directions, form locally. Waves which travel for some distance become regular swells with parallel crests. (Although energy moves forward in the form of waves, individual water molecules remain in the same place, describing a small, circular path near the surface.)

Wave energy continues to move forward until it encounters an obstacle. If the obstacle were a long, straight, unprotected shoreline, which the wave struck head on, a long straight beach would result. Such

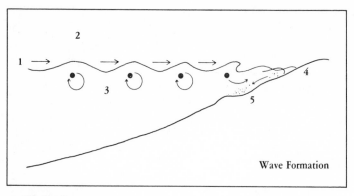

Wave Formation

1. Wind strikes water
2. Energy moves forward
3. Water molecules remain in place
4. Swash — water, sand, driftwood, and shells are carried on to the beach
5. Backwash

is not the case in Maine. Waves bump into hundreds of shoals, islands, and peninsulas which influence their direction, velocity, and force. Since Maine beaches were generally formed parallel to approaching waves, the state's sandy areas are aligned with respect to wave refraction patterns, or bending. A single bay may have beaches which face south, east, and west, but each beach lies parallel to incoming waves.

Beach Profile

Waves not only determine the alignment of a beach, they also determine its cross-sectional profile. But in order to understand this aspect, it is necessary to first describe the parts of a beach. The beach is divided into the offshore, foreshore, backshore and dunes (see next page). The offshore is always covered with water. Shoaling waves form here, and sediments often accumulate in an offshore bar paralleled by a trough. The foreshore includes the intertidal zone, where waves sweep over the sand. The backshore extends from mean high water level to the frontal dune ridge, while dunes encompass the sandy area from the ridge to a lagoon, marsh or upland area.

As a wave moves into the shallow offshore, it slows down and becomes steeper. When the height of the wave equals the depth of the water, the wave can no longer hold its shape and breaks into a swirl of foam, the swash. At this point, water molecules no longer stay in place

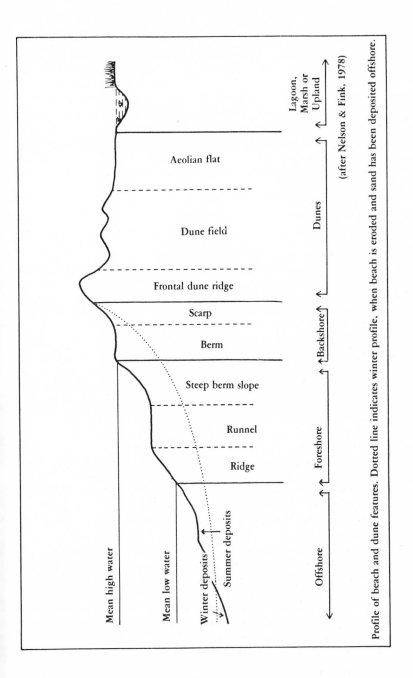

Profile of beach and dune features. Dotted line indicates winter profile, when beach is eroded and sand has been deposited offshore.

(after Nelson & Fink, 1978)

but are carried up the beach, along with sand, seaweed, shells and other debris. The strength of the wave determines whether the sand remains on the beach face or is carried back to the offshore by the backwash. High energy waves may take away more sand than they bring, causing erosion of the beach face. Typically, summer waves have low energy and deposit sand along the intertidal zone, creating a summer berm or terrace. Sometimes a second terrace or ridge also forms on the lower foreshore paralleled by a shallow channel called a runnel. High energy winter storm waves (usually northeasters) erode these terraces, forming a steeply sloped scarp next to the frontal dune ridge and transporting sand offshore.

Dunes

Dune fields complete the profile of most Maine beaches. They, too, are divided into sections. The frontal dune ridge separates the backshore from the backdune and protects this interior area from wave action. Dune ridges are found on almost all undeveloped beaches but are noticeably absent on beaches with seawalls or heavy, unrestricted foot. travel. Interior dunes and aeolian flats (flat, sparsely vegetated areas) make up the remainder of the dune field. Parabolic dunes are a special form. As wind redistributes sand, a U-shaped feature is created, a feature which is capable of migrating downwind. Maine is unique because its parabolic dunes are formed by strong winds blowing offshore from the northwest, as opposed to winds blowing onshore which dominate in most other states. Good examples of stabilized parabolic dunes may be seen at Popham and Reid Beaches. Repeated parabolic dune activity and stabilization by vegetation create the hummocky topography of backdune areas.

Dunes are much more than windswept mounds of sand. Dune formation depends on the unique adaptations of American beachgrass (*Ammophila breviligulata*), which is generally the dominant cover plant. When a shoot of *Ammophila* is washed ashore after winter erosion, it roots and sends up new grass blades. It also sends out rhizomes, horizontal runners which spread like spokes in a wheel. Every six to ten inches along the runner, the plant sets more roots and sprouts. An intertwined network of roots, runners, and plants develops.

Once established, *Ammophila* begins to actively trap sand which is being blown by the wind from the dry supratidal zone. Sand accumulates. But rather than being killed by sand burial, *Ammophila* is stimulated to further growth. The plant pushes above the surface. In addition to the vertical growth, it sends out a new lattice-work of runners, parallel to but above the old network. As the plant grows, more sand is trapped, and more growth results, until a balance between sand, wind and vegetation is reached. Below the surface, an interconnecting mass of roots, rhizomes and buried plants stabilizes the sand and creates the basis for dunes. Particular forms and features found in a dune field depend on local wind and sand conditions.

The above description accounts for the historical development of dune fields in Maine. Like beaches, dune fields have generally reached a state of equilibrium (though again, this does not mean that dunes do not change shape). Although wind continues to shape the fields, it no longer brings large amounts of sand from the backshore into the backdune, but rather the sand accumulates on the frontal dune ridge. Major sand transport into the backdune area is caused by winter storm waves which overwash or breach the frontal dune ridge, depositing a layer of sand which, in turn, stimulates widespread growth of *Ammophila*. Overwash is one method of compensating for sea level rise. Even an inch of sand transferred from the foreshore to the dunes can compensate for many decades of sea level rise.

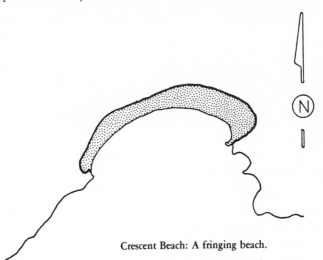

Crescent Beach: A fringing beach.

Beach Types in Maine

Beaches are classified according to what they look like. *Fringing beaches* usually lie next to bedrock or soil and do not have extensive dune fields or an interior lagoon. Parts of Old Orchard Beach and Crescent Beach in southern Maine are examples of large fringing beaches.

Pocket fringing beaches, such as Crescent Beach in Cape Elizabeth and part of Sandy River Beach in Jonesport, are found at the heads of bays (therefore, between two nearby headlands) and are characteristically small and curved.

Barrier beaches are attached to the mainland at both ends, may or may not include a tidal inlet behind the beach, but always protect a lagoon or a lagoon-turned-salt marsh. Mile Beach at Reid illustrates this type. Smaller pocket barrier beaches are quite common and include Sea Point, Pemaquid, Sand Beach, and Roque Bluffs.

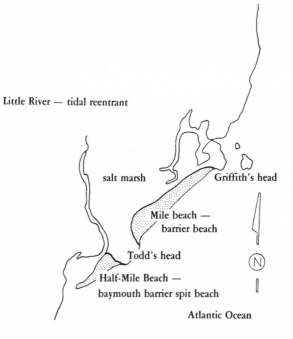

Little River — tidal reentrant

salt marsh

Griffith's head

Mile beach —
barrier beach

Todd's head

Half-Mile Beach —
baymouth barrier spit beach

Atlantic Ocean

Reid State Park

Barrier spit beaches extend partway across a bay mouth and are associated with a long straight dune field, a tidal inlet, and a salt marsh. Ogunquit, part of Goose Rocks, Scarborough, and Half Mile Beach at Reid State Park are all baymouth barrier spit beaches. The presence of these spits indicates some movement of sand parallel to the shore, although this movement is small relative to downdrifting along large beaches which stretch south from Massachusetts.

The tidal inlet which is found with barrier spit beaches and some other barrier beaches is more than a simple channel. Typically, sand which was carried by tidal water into the mouth of the inlet was deposited, rather than being carried back to the offshore. If this sand is considered erosional material (that is, coming from the land), then it "re-entered" the inlet and the channel is termed a reentrant. Once an equilibrium is reached, the transfer no longer occurs. Sand deposits in a reentrant may become large enough to act as sand supply for dune fields. Rear dune ridges, an uncommon form in Maine, develop from wind-blown sand derived from reentrants.

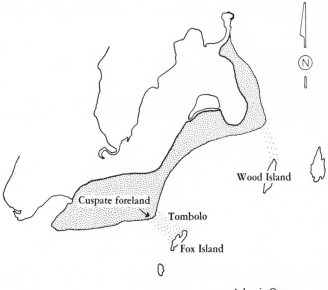

Popham Beach

Tombolos are small beaches or bars running between two islands or connecting one island with the mainland. The bars may be exposed only at low tide. Tombolos have formed in the lee of Fox Island and Wood Island at Popham State Park. Popham also illustrates cuspate forelands, large seaward projections of beach and dune which often form (as they do here) at one end of tombolos.

Life at the Beach

The same factors which limit life on the rocky shore pose boundaries to dwellers of the beach. Potential inhabitants must contend with wind, salt, inundation, and an even greater challenge: lack of a stable substrate. Holdfasts, byssal threads, suction cups, and sticky mucus are to no avail and the beach is relatively barren of full-time residents.

But close inspection along the lower foreshore reveals one set of animals which have adapted to these conditions. Burrowing worms, ghost shrimp, beach hoppers, clams, starfish and crabs use the damp sand for protection and feed when covered with water. But they cannot survive the hot, dry sands of the backshore, and little animal life except insects and mice can be found there.

No plants grow on the lower, drifting beach, although plants have adapted to the heat, desiccation, and salt spray of the berm and dune. American beachgrass, dusty miller, sea rocket and saltwort are plants common to beaches but not found in other ecosystems. Lichens, seaside goldenrod, beach pea, sea blite, seaside rose, orach, pitch pine, and more than eighty other species are found on the berm and on dunes, as well as in other coastal habitats.

Birds

A yearly sequence of birds frequent the sandy beach. Shorebirds migrate through Maine in May en route to nesting grounds on the tundra. Piping plover, spotted sandpiper, gulls and terns can be seen during the summer. Shorebirds return from the north July-November, depending on the species. In winter the purple sandpiper, gulls, offshore ducks, loons and grebes (see Rocky Shore list) are the common avifauna.

Shorebirds

Semipalmated plover	Common, May, Aug-Sept
Piping plover	Uncommon, summer
Black-bellied plover	Common, May, Aug-Oct

Ruddy turnstone	Common, May, Aug-Oct
Spotted sandpiper	Common, summer
Greater yellowlegs	Common, May, Aug-Sept
Lesser yellowlegs	Common, August
Purple sandpiper	Common, Nov-March
Pectoral sandpiper	Common, Sept
Least sandpiper	Common, May, Aug-Sept
Dunlin	Common, Sept-Oct
Short-billed dowitcher	Common, May, July-Sept
Semipalmated sandpiper	Common, May, Aug-Sept
Sanderling	Common, July-Sept
Gulls	
Great black-backed	Common, resident
Herring	Common, resident
Ring-billed	Common, Sept-Oct
Laughing	Uncommon, May-Sept
Terns	
Common	Common, May-Aug
Arctic	Common, May-Aug
Roseate	Uncommon, June-Aug
Least	Uncommon, May-Aug
Savannah sparrow	Common, May-Sept
	(nests in dune grass)

The least tern is one of Maine's rarest breeding species. An estimated 120 birds nest on the flat, sparsely vegetated or bare berm, relatively close to the high tide line. Often, they breed near small tidal rivers to ensure a food supply. Also, the sparsely vegetated berm broadens near the spit end, providing a larger nesting habitat. This very specific nesting habitat eliminates all but a half-dozen sites in the state and even then birds are exposed to numerous predators and harassment by beach visitors. Least terns are known to abandon the nest when disturbed, although they will frequently attempt to renest at another suitable spot. Three nesting areas, including Popham Beach, have been included in the Register of Critical Areas for the state. Most sites have been posted, asking visitors to avoid the region between May 15 and July 15.

Piping plover is also uncommon in Maine and is often seen nesting with least terns. Plover prefers similar habitat except that it nests nearer the dune ridge and is less susceptible to damage by storm waves. Five sites, including Wells and Popham Beach, are registered as Critical Areas for piping plover; the birds also nest at Ogunquit Beach, near the snow fence which protects the dunes.

The Beach and People

Heavy development has encroached on more than half of Maine's coastal dune regions. Ogunquit, Moody, Wells, Drakes Island, Kennebunk, Goose Rocks, Fortunes Rocks, Saco, Old Orchard and Higgins Beaches have been dramatically altered, and many of the significant dune formations have been obliterated. Some dune areas are now protected by fences and signs, but they are still liable to damage when visitors leave the marked paths and cut across the fields.

The relationship between humans and natural systems often determines the character of the process involved. For example, shoreline change is a normal response to rising sea level. No one was concerned—in fact, few people noticed—when the sand beach at Popham receded over 500 feet between 1940 and 1972. But thousands of individuals noticed the much smaller amount of erosion at Hunnewell Beach. The difference is that houses line Hunnewell, while Popham has none.

The process was termed destructive and, in a sense, it was. Houses toppled into the surf. But as they did, philosophical questions emerged. Is not erosion "destructive" only in relation to humans? If erosion is seen as a change, rather than destruction, what differences in approach would result? In effect, how can humans live in harmony with natural changes so that loss of personal property does not result?

Further Reading and Reference

The Face of North America by Peter Farb (Harper and Fow, Publishers, Inc., 1963). An excellent survey book describing various major ecosystems of North America.

Geological and Botanical Features of Sand Beach Systems in Maine by Bruce Nelson and L. Kenneth Fink, Jr. (State Planning Office, 1978). A very good technical text.

The Life of the Seashore by William Amos (McGraw-Hill Book Company, 1966). Excellent introduction and overview.

The Winter Beach by Charlton Ogburn (Morrow, 1966). Identification guide.

Freshwater Wetlands

They come to Maine as early as late February, cutting through the gray winter sky with deep, powerful wing beats. Their honking sounds through the crisp air: loud, plaintive, urging. They appear above the trees in an irregular V, an arrangement which lends protection and strength to the entire number. At dusk, they settle into small marshes to feed and rest, eating grass sprouts, grains and marine vegetation. The proud black head, marked by white cheek patches, is always alert to danger and intruders.

The Canada goose is perhaps the best known and most cherished of all the animals which frequent Maine's freshwater regions, and that full list is long and varied. The human inhabitants have long depended on these animals for food, clothing and livelihood. Indians and settlers hunted deer, bear, ducks, geese and other species, all of which were plentiful in coastal regions. Fur became an early commodity of trade and a mainstay of the state's economy. The search for one mammal in particular—the beaver—opened vast new areas to traders and entrepreneurs.

Today, different economic factors come into play. Wetlands store water and help prevent flooding. They bind pollutants—chemical fertilizers, pesticides, heavy metals, sewage—into their biological system and thus cleanse ground water. They provide recreation to thousands of nature lovers, canoeists, hunters, and trappers. To the scientist, they represent one ephemeral moment in the evolution of the earth, a valuable case study in succession.

How are wetlands created? What is their place in the natural cycle? The answers begin, as usual, with the glacier.

From Pond to Woodland

The landscape was barren 10,000 years ago. Great chunks of ice were scattered over the countryside and water filled numerous basins gouged out of bedrock. Ponds and lakes spread across New England. But almost immediately, sedimentation began filling in those lakes, and succession—the orderly replacement of one plant community with another—began to change open bodies of water to bogs, marshes and swamps and later to woodland.

Freshwater wetlands are generally classified by vegetation and environment. If the area is highly acidic, has stagnant or slow moving water, is covered by a layer of sphagnum moss, and has few nutrients, it is a bog. If it consists of grasses, sedges, and rushes, but no trees; if it has moving water and a good supply of minerals, it is a marsh. If the region has trees and shrubs as well as moving water and many nutrients, it is a swamp. The typical sequence of change from one habitat to another is: pond—marsh—swamp—forest.

Ponds and lakes are natural traps for stream-born sediments. As sediments accumulate, bottom-dwelling plants root in shallow areas and emergent plants such as cattails and rushes grow along the edges. Plants die and they too become "fill." Eventually, a shallow marsh replaces open water. Streams continue to bring sediments and nutrients to the area. Water-tolerant trees move in, changing the region to a swamp. Trees pull water from the moist earth, allowing upland species to crowd closer, and eventually the former pond is covered with woods. Light, soil, nutrients, and exposure influence succession and the precise nature of each area, so that this sequence is more of a general progression than an exact description for every wetland.

Maine has some notable areas of marshland. Merrymeeting Bay, for example, clearly illustrates the process of sedimentation and marsh formation. But most of Maine's sediments were cleared away by glacial ice. Instead of a pond-marsh-swamp-forest sequence, the many nutrient-poor kettleholes encourage a similar but separate process, whereby ponds evolve into bogs and then—sometimes—into forests. Major swamps and marshes are located in the mid-Atlantic and southeastern United States, while bogs are characteristic of northern, post-glaciated areas.

Bogs

Bogs are sterile, self-contained environments. The underlying bedrock, usually granite, supplies few minerals. Little or no moving water brings correspondingly few new nutrients. Calcium, phosphorus, oxygen, and nitrogen are in especially short supply. The lack of oxygen prevents aerobic decomposition and peat bogs characteristically contain large quantities of undecomposed matter. Arctic and tropical plants, both of which are well adapted to a nutrient-poor, acidic environment,

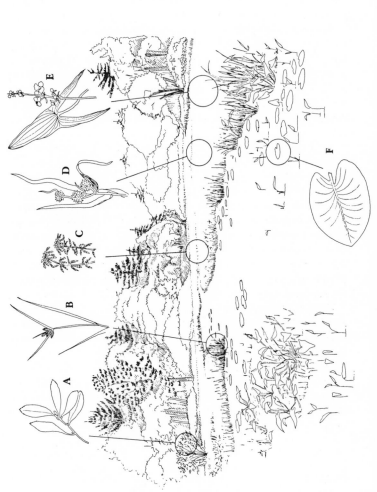

Plant life in a young bog. (A) Sweet gale (B) Sedge (C) Sphagnum moss (D) Burred reed (E) Arrowhead (F) Water lily

grow well in this habitat, but swamp and marsh species are noticeably absent.

The change from pond to bog occurs over many years. Water lilies and other aquatic plants colonize the surface of the pond. Pioneer species such as cotton grass, buckbean, and shrubs vegetate the pond's edge. Sphagnum moss develops within the structure afforded by the shrubs. Sphagnum is a key plant, as it depletes the water of oxygen, calcium, and nitrogen and absorbs great quantities of water in special cask-like cells. It can hold up to twenty times its weight in water, hoarding the few minerals made available through rain water. The moss continues to grow, expanding upward and outward, pushing old growth under water and eventually creating a floating mat of vegetation. The quaking bog which sags when stepped on is typical of this state of succession.

As the sphagnum layers built up and out, sheep laurel, labrador tea and leatherleaf take root in the somewhat dryer substrate. When the mat grows to the edge of the pond, it can spill out into the woods, for the sphagnum moss holds water to such a degree that it can create its own water table above the normal water level. If the bog continues to expand, the encompassed vegetation will die because it cannot tolerate the sterile environment. Several bogs in eastern Maine are expanding in this manner. Toward the end of this consolidation phase, water tolerant trees—American white cedar on the coast and black spruce and larch inland—take root and produce a forested peatland.

Some ecologists feel that the bog is a climax community, that the peat, shrubs, spruce, and smaller bog plants are uniquely suited to the growing conditions and they will not be replaced by other vegetation unless there is a change in the system, for example, a shift in the ground water. Other ecologists feel that in time the bog will fill in and black spruce or cedar will completely take over, pumping out water and drying the peat substrate. Both theories seem to be true for different situations. Some bogs which developed shortly after the retreat of the glacier survive to this day, while others have grown into forest.

Both arctic and tropical species have adaptations suited to survival in Maine's bogs. The high pH makes it difficult for vegetation to use otherwise abundant moisture, and northern plants such as labrador tea, bog laurel, and leatherleaf have either wooly or waxy leaves which retard the loss of water vapor. Tropical vegetation—pitcher plants and sundew—live independent of the nutrient-poor substrate by trapping insects for food.

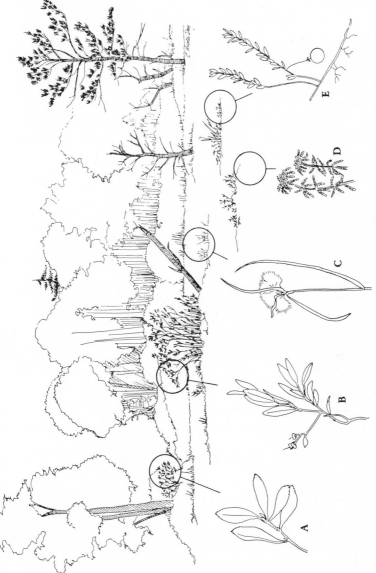

Plant life in a mature bog. (A) Sweet gale (B) Leather leaf (C) Cottongrass (D) Sphagnum moss (E) Wren's egg cranberry

Bogs and Boogeymen

While lumbermen vied for virgin white pine, bogs and heaths of Maine were left largely untouched. This may have resulted from an inherited mistrust of wetland areas which Europeans have harbored since Grendel emerged from the evil heath in *Beowulf*. Even language reflects these fears. "Heathen" refers to non-Christian barbarians who lived on the English heaths and moors. Spirits stalked the heath at night in *Hamlet*. "Boogeymen" originally described demons from the bog.

But somehow, the mystique has vanished. Bogs are viewed from a more practical standpoint. Peat has been used for energy for centuries in Ireland. Maine has several large heaths with minable peat which could be used for fuel and horticulture. However, these heaths also protect a variety of wildlife and a number of rare and unusual plants, in addition to providing recreational opportunities. Although peat mining is a relatively nonpolluting process, it has not yet been determined whether mining, wildlife, and recreation are compatible, and, if not, which should be given priority.

Wetland Birds

Although a large number of these birds nest in Maine, most are seen during spring and fall migrations.

Bitterns	
Least	Uncommon, summer
American	Common, summer
Waterfowl	
Canada goose	Common, migrant
Mallard	Uncommon, resident
Black duck	Common, resident
Pintail	Common, migrant
Blue-winged teal	Common, summer
Green-winged teal	Common, summer
American wigeon	Common, migrant
Wood duck	Common, summer
Ring-necked duck	Common, summer
Greater scaup	Common, winter
Common goldeneye	Common, winter
Hooded merganser	Uncommon, summer
Common merganser	Common, year round

Red-breasted merganser	Common, Sept-April
Bald eagle	Uncommon, resident
Osprey	Common, summer
Cranes and Allies	
Virginia rail	Common, summer
Sora	Common, summer
Common gallinule	Uncommon, summer
American coot	Uncommon, summer
Greater yellowlegs	Common, migrant
Yellow-bellied flycatcher	Common, summer
Long-billed marsh wren	Common, summer
Warblers	
Tennessee warbler	Common, summer
Nashville warbler	Common, summer
Palm warbler or parula	Uncommon, summer
Northern waterthrush	Common, summer
Yellow-throated warbler	Common, summer
Blackbirds	
Red-winged blackbird	Common, March-Oct
Rusty blackbird	Common, summer
Common grackle	Common, March-Nov

Animals in and Around Freshwater Wetlands

ANIMAL	Notes about habitat or locale. Unless otherwise indicated, range extends all along coast.
Shrews	
Masked shrew	Moist situations, stream bottoms
Short-tailed shrew	Marshes
Starnose mole	Wet meadows and marshes, low wet ground near lakes
Raccoon	Along streams and lakes of wooded area
Weasels	
Short-tailed weasel (ermine)	Brushy or wooded area not far from water
Long-tailed weasel	All land habitat near water
Mink	Along streams and lakes, flowages, impoundments
River otter	Main waterways and lake borders
Gray fox	Swamp as well as open forest of southern Maine
Bobcat	Swamp and forest of remote areas
Red squirrel	Swamp
Beaver	Streams and lakes with trees or alders on banks

Rodents

Southern bog lemming	Low damp bogs and meadows
Meadow vole	Near streams, lakes, swamps
Muskrat	Aquatic
Meadow jumping mouse	Marsh lands and meadows
Woodland jumping mouse	Wet bogs, stream borders

Deer

White-tailed deer	Swamps, especially cedar swamps
Moose	Swamps, along rivers

Further Reading and Reference

"Bogs," by Edward Deevey, *Scientific American* (Volume 199, #4, October 1958)

Life in and Around Freshwater Wetlands by Michael Ursin (Thomas Y. Crowell Company, 1975). Introduction to wetlands and identification of common plants and animals.

The Life of the Marsh by William Niering (McGraw Hill Company, 1966). Comprehensive text of marsh environment.

The Life of a Pond by William Amos (McGraw Hill Company, 1967). Comprehensive text of marsh environment.

FROM KITTERY TO EASTPORT

The coast naturally divides into three large sections. The southern portion sweeps from Kittery to Portland and is characterized by long beaches (by Maine standards) and salt marshes. Tall white pines are dominant on the sandy soil. At one time, saltwater farms lined the shore and farmers harvested salt marsh grass for fodder and thatch. Because of its proximity to major population centers in New England, the southern coast is the most heavily developed and populated area of the state.

From Portland to Ellsworth—the area which encompasses Casco and Penobscot Bays—lies a deeply indented coastline. Protected coves, inlets, reaches and necks are common. Pocket beaches and small salt marshes are tucked into hundreds of headlands and crevices. Island communities make up a unique way of life, where taking the ferry is as normal as taking the bus.

"Downeast" indicates different areas to different people, but certainly the stretch north and east of Ellsworth differs from the rest of the coast. It is a land of spruce-fir forest, a land of high tides, a land where arctic plants grow close to the ocean. The towns Downeast are small and relatively isolated, and the residents generally like them that way.

Kittery-Kennebunk

Fort Foster

Fort Foster, built in 1872, is the southernmost point in Maine and guards the entrance to Portsmouth Harbor. The now-abandoned bunkers provide a backdrop for a large park operated by the town of Kittery. The park has several small, polished stone beaches, a nature trail through mixed hardwoods, and picnic areas. Fort Foster is a good site for watching wintering ducks. All the common species, as well as Barrow's goldeneye, are regularly reported. Migrating shore birds pass through the area from mid-July to October, and migrating land birds (warblers, thrushes, sparrows and nuthatches) are plentiful.

The exposed rocks along the shore are metamorphosed igneous rocks, primarily metafelsite. Felsite is a fine-grained volcanic rock which formed 500 million years ago during the Taconic mountain-building period. Later crustal movement during the Acadian Orogeny changed the crystalline structure, creating meta (short for metamorphosed) felsite.

A small, lettered stone in the cemetery opposite the Congregational Church at Kittery Point marks the grave of six men who drowned when their ship, the *Hattie Eaton*, foundered on Garrish Island. Shipwrecks were common in the treacherous area bounded by the Pisquatiqua River, Cape Neddick Nubble, Boon Island (6½ miles southeast of Cape Neddick), and Isles of Shoals (southeast of Portsmouth). Between 110 and 200 ships wrecked on the shallow ledges and rocks. The most famous incident occurred in 1710 on a stormy December day. The *Nottingham Galley* out of England smashed against Boon Island. Although the survivors could see ships going in and out of Portsmouth Harbor, they were unable to attract attention. The chilling story is preserved in *Boon Island*, one of Kenneth Roberts' many historical novels about Maine.

> From Kittery, take Rte. 103 east for 2 miles. Turn right onto Chauncey Creek Road at sign for Fort Foster. Drive ½ mile to Garrish Island Bridge. Cross bridge, turn right, and follow road 1.2 miles to Fort Foster Park. Fee $1 per person.

Map 1 Kittery-Kennebunk

Seapoint

Seapoint is a tiny peninsula which juts into the Atlantic, separating Sea-point Beach and Crescent Beach. The beaches have no dunes but are backed by a small marsh which attracts several species of heron, glossy ibis, snowy egret and, upon occasion, common egret. Shorebirds are common in the late summer and ducks winter by the point. Seapoint is not a large recreational facility but a small area primarily known to bird-watchers.

Continue on Chauncey Creek Road 1 mile past the Garrish Island Bridge. Bear right when the road forks. Limited parking. Free.

Sohier Park

Sohier Park is a small area of well-exposed gabbro, an intrusion which occurred during the Acadian Orogony and has since been exposed by erosion. Gabbro is a dark-colored, very tough igneous rock which resists weathering. Sohier Park is located on the eastern tip of Cape Neddick and is another good winter birding area. In addition to the common winter ducks, sightings include harlequin duck, king eider, Barrow's goldeneye, and gannets. Cape Neddick Nubble, a federally operated lighthouse, lies just offshore.

Stay on Rte. 1A south through York Beach. When the road comes to a T, turn left (toward Chamber of Commerce) and take first right onto Broadway. Follow road ½ mile to lighthouse. Free admission.

Vaughan Woods

Vaughan Woods, on the banks of the Salmon Falls River, is a 250-acre state park with 2-3 miles of secluded trails and a picnic area. The river trail runs through a beautiful hemlock wood. The ship "The Pied Cow" landed in Cow Cove at the southern end of the park in 1634. It brought the first cows to this section of the state as well as the first sawmill, which was set up nearby. Vaughan Woods is an excellent site for birdwatching during the land bird migrations in spring and fall. The secretive piliated woodpecker may sometimes be seen. The park's trails are good for snowshoeing and cross-country skiing as well as hiking.

From Kittery, travel north on Rte. 236 about 9½ miles. Turn west on Rte. 91, follow it until it comes to a T, and then turn left. Continue for 1 mile to park entrance. Free.

Ferns in woods.

Perkins Cove and Marginal Way

Marginal Way is a ½-mile paved path which follows the rocky shore just south of Ogunquit. It is not a route through the wilderness, but it has been thoughtfully planned to skirt residences and allow visitors access to the beautiful ocean view. Several lunching, thinking and resting benches are located along the route, and in summertime it is a favorite and much-used trail.

Dieback of juniper and cedar to the west of the path indicate the extent of salt spray along the shore. The upturned metamorphic rocks are a graphic illustration of the crushing and deformity which occurred in this area 350 million years ago. Migrating birds frequent the cove in season and, during the winter months, ducks (sometimes even harlequin duck!) may be seen.

Traveling north on Rte. 1, take a sharp right in the center of Ogunquit onto Shore Road. Continue for 1 mile to Perkins Cove, a development of shops and houses. Marginal Way begins at the northeast corner of the parking lot. Free.

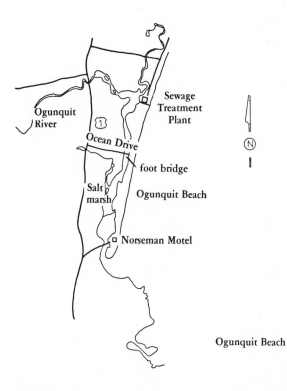

Ogunquit Beach

Ogunquit Beach

Ogunquit and Moody Beaches form the largest barrier spit beach, tidal river, and marsh system in the state. Although the Moody section is crowded with houses and businesses, the stretch between the Norseman Hotel and the sewage treatment plant is a valuable and beautiful area. Ogunquit is known for its dazzling white and fine-grained sand. The sand, almost pure quartz grains, has been winnowed by glacial meltwater streams and then waves. The beach is a textbook example of summer-versus-winter profile. The summer berm is wide and smooth (which also makes it a favorite swimming and sunning beach), while the winter waves transfer sand to the offshore region and leave the winter berm much narrower.

The dune field between the Norseman Hotel and the sewage treatment plant formerly contained the largest and most active parabolic dunes in the state. American beachgrass, beach pea, and wormwood form the vegetative cover, for only the heartiest plants have been able to withstand the strong northwest wind and previous pedestrian travel. The dunes themselves are badly eroded, and it is difficult to pick out the classic parabolic shape. To protect the area, a twelve-foot high sand and gravel dike has been constructed along the upper edge of the beach, and the entire area is encircled by a snowfence. The dike is planted with neat rows of American beachgrass—a contrast to the random growth of wild grass nearby.

Ogunquit is especially nice early in the morning and in the off season. The sand beach and salt marsh provide two different but nearby ecosystems for birders and botanists. Usual shore and marsh birds have been sighted, in addition to less usual glossy ibises migrating south in September.

> One mile north of the center of Ogunquit turn east on Ocean Drive. Parking is either free (½ hour) or by fee ($3 per day in the summer). The footbridge crosses over the marsh and dunes and enters the beach north of the motel.

Mount Agamenticus

Mount Agamenticus is a significant botanical landmark, for it is the northern boundary for many southern plant species. Chestnut oak, black birch, flowering dogwood and spleenwort do not grow north of this region. In fact, flowering dogwood grows nowhere else in the state and is therefore classified as rare, though it is common in southern New England. Two stands of dogwood were cleared for the observation tower many years before Mount Agamenticus was identified as the single growing site for the species.

Maine's Critical Areas Program (part of the State Planning Office) was created in 1974 to locate and identify significant natural areas—like Mount Agamenticus—and to encourage their protection. The program does not regulate land use, but coordinates conservation efforts. Many times simply informing landowners of the presence of unusual plants, birds, mammals, or geological formations serves to protect the feature. Further information about the program can be obtained by contacting:

State Planning Office
Critical Areas Program
184 State Street
Augusta, Maine 04333

Mount Agamenticus was developed as a ski resort, but the business did not prosper. Although the abandoned buildings do not add to the view, the summit does provide an outstanding perch to look at the surrounding countryside. It is also a good site to view the migrating hawks in the fall.

0.3 miles south of Ogunquit turn off Rte. 1 and onto Agamenticus Road. Continue 3.9 miles, turn right at the T, and follow the road for 1.6 more miles. Turn right at the sign for the ski area. Free.

Wells Harbor and Webhannet River Marsh

The harbor and marsh are rich in ducks, shorebirds, and marsh birds. Glossy ibis, snowy egret, and several species of heron summer in the marsh. During the fall shorebird migration, black-bellied and semipalmated plovers, dunlin, short-billed dowitcher, killdeer, greater and lesser yellowlegs, and three species of sandpipers are often seen. The marsh is a nesting site for the piping plover (rare in Maine), killdeer, horned lark, and savannah sparrow. A short-eared owl lives nearby. Ducks, loons, grebes, great cormorant, and three species of gulls winter in the area. Several sightings of thick-billed murre and common murre have been reported from the harbor.

From the center of Wells, turn east toward the harbor. Free.

Rachael Carson National Wildlife Refuge

The Rachael Carson Refuge is a series of wetlands which run along the entire Atlantic seaboard. The areas protect migrating waterfowl and are administered by the U.S. Fish and Wildlife Service. They were named in honor of Rachael Carson, whose writings, including *Silent Spring* and *The Edge of the Sea*, initiated a movement toward environmental consciousness and conservation. The refuge in Wells includes a white pine forest which opens onto a large salt marsh. The pines harbor a host of land birds, including red-breasted and white-breasted nuthatches, black-capped chickadee, hairy and downy woodpeckers, tufted titmouse, and a variety of vireos and warblers. Herons, egrets, kingfisher, glossy ibis and shorebirds (in season) may be seen in the marsh. Several paths lead through the pines and onto the marsh, forming a one mile circle trip. Mosquito season lasts from spring through fall (even frost does not deter the insects) and visitors should come prepared.

At juncture of Rte. 1 and Rte. 9 north of Wells, turn east on Rte. 9 for 0.7 miles. Park by the side of the road on either side of the refuge sign. Free admission.

Kennebunk-Portland

Goose Rocks Beach and Fortunes Rocks Beach

Both of these beaches have lost many of their unique features—particularly the dune fields—as a result of development. Both areas, however, attract birds as well as bird watchers. Osprey, marsh hawk, and belted kingfisher are often seen in the Baston River salt marsh, which lies behind the spit at the southwest end of Goose Rocks Beach. In 1977, least terns nested on the spit, establishing a new nesting area in the state. The site was posted and protected, and the birds have subsequently returned.

Common, arctic, and roseate terns dive for fish along both Goose Rocks Beach and Fortunes Rocks Beach and ducks commonly winter offshore. Across the road from Fortunes Rocks, Lily Pond provides a stopping-over site for migrating bay ducks. Ring-necked duck, ruddy duck, black duck, mallard, bufflehead, scaup, green-winged teal, blue-winged teal, American coot, and pied-billed grebe have all been reported.

Follow Rte. 9 from Kennebunkport (through Cape Porpoise) for 9 miles. Turn east at the sign for Goose Rocks Beach and continue 1 mile to the town. To get to Fortunes Rocks Beach, continue on Rte. 9 for 2 ½ miles north of the Goose Rocks turn-off. Turn right at the sign for Fortunes Rocks. Lily Pond is ½ mile on the left. Free admission.

Biddeford Pool

The Biddeford Pool-East Point Sanctuary area is the best location for birding in southern Maine. The two nearby sites provide quite different habitats. Large mudflats at the pool attract thousands of migrating shorebirds, while ducks, pelagic (sea-going) birds, and land birds appear at East Point. An afternoon of birding in September can be no less than exciting, for it is not unusual to see twenty or more species.

The pool itself is a basin one mile in diameter which empties out of the northeast corner. Low tide exposes many acres of mudflats to pip-

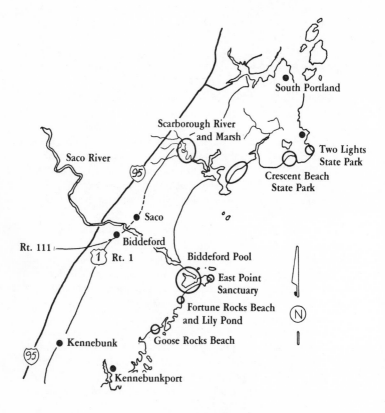

South Portland

Scarborough River
and Marsh

Saco River

Two Lights
State Park

95

Crescent Beach
State Park

Saco

Rt. 111

Biddeford

Biddeford Pool

1 Rt. 1

East Point
Sanctuary

Fortune Rocks Beach
and Lily Pond

N

Kennebunk

Goose Rocks Beach

95

Kennebunkport

Map 2 Kennebunk-Portland

ing, golden, and black-bellied plovers; Hudsonian godwit; whimbrel; and three species of sandpipers (Baird's, buff-breasted, and pectoral). Unusual sightings include marbled godwit, avocet, ruff sandpiper, and curlew sandpiper. The ideal time to birdwatch is about 1 ½ hours before high tide, when the birds are concentrated in a fringe of mudflats near dry land.

Take Rte. 9/208 south out of Biddeford for 5 miles (or follow Rte. 9 north from Kennebunkport). Turn east on Rte. 208. The road follows the edge of the pool. Free.

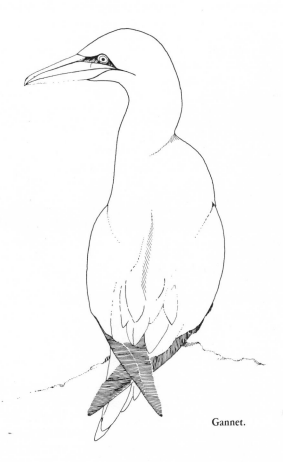

Gannet.

East Point Sanctuary

East Point Sanctuary, acquired in 1976 by the Maine Audubon Society, is a 30-acre tract which includes several pebble beaches, an open field, and a trail network. It is a very good site for watching spring and fall migrations and wintering birds. King eider and Barrow's goldeneye are frequently observed among the common ducks during the winter months. Purple sandpiper and occasionally ruddy turnstones are also seen. Because it juts into the ocean, East Point is a likely spot to observe pelagic birds which have been blown toward shore. Alcids such as dovekie, black guillemot, common murre, and thick-billed murre have been seen. Gannet, a relative of the pelican, has also been reported. The woods near the golf course attract unusual song birds, such as the western kingbird, and a variety of warblers and sparrows.

Follow Rte. 208 past Biddeford Pool to the intersection of 208 (which becomes Main Street) and Ocean Avenue. Park along Ocean Ave. Parking space is limited. Walk back on Main about 30 yards. A chain link gate fronts an old dirt road. Follow the worn path around the gate and up the road along the golf course. Access to the sanctuary is by foot only and the Maine Audubon Society requests that the area remain a sanctuary rather than a picnic or recreation area. Free admission.

Scarborough Marsh

Scarborough is the largest salt marsh in Maine. The 3000-acre tract is not only a lovely area, it also offers a well-developed recreational and educational program. In conjunction with the Department of Inland Fisheries and Wildlife, which administers the sanctuary, the Maine Audubon Society runs a summer nature center. Visitor activities include daily marsh walks, twice-a-week guided canoe trips, rental canoes for independent exploration, exhibits, a slide show, and an aquarium. The staff also leads programs at nearby beaches to investigate marine ecology.

The Nature Center is open from May until the end of September, but the marsh is available to the public year round. Scarborough is an excellent place to look for animal tracks, study salt marsh ecology, and watch for birds. Early spring ducks include common, red-breasted and hooded mergansers; black duck; canvasback; widgeon; mallard; blue-winged and green-winged teals; and an occasional pintail. Great flocks of Canada geese and sometimes smaller numbers of snow geese feed in the salt marsh cord grass, taking a brief rest from the arduous flight to summer breeding grounds. Herons, egrets, glossy ibis, American bit-

Orach.

tern, woodcock, common snipe, sora, Virginia rail, song sparrow, sharp-tailed sparrow, and long-billed marsh wren are all also commonly seen.

At the juncture of Rte. 1 and Rte. 9 in West Scarborough, turn southeast on Pine Point Road (Rte. 9). The center is 1½ miles on the left. Free admission.

Scarborough Beach State Park

Scarborough Beach is a closed barrier beach fronting a freshwater marsh called Massacre Pond. Geologists think that in the past—perhaps 4000 years ago—the beach was an open barrier which protected a lagoon and salt marsh. Since then, sea level has risen, build-up of sand has closed the inlet, and sand dunes have moved over the old marsh. A few low relief parabolic dunes near the access road are thickly vegetated with American beachgrass. The strong onshore winds have sprayed salt on trees and shrubs which line the backdune, creating a dieback and noticeable flagging, or wind pruning, of trees.

The southwest and middle stretches of the beach are clearly eroded, while the northeast end is built up. Natural forces are at work.

Southwest winds may be creating a longshore current (a current which moves parallel to the beach face), which in turn carries sand to the northern end of the beach. Or approaching waves may hit the beach at an angle, sweeping the sand along toward the far end. Although it may seem to make little difference in this case which force is responsible for sand transport, such questions become critical issues when applied to large scale erosion involving private and public property. Studying small areas such as Scarborough Beach gives insights to larger and more complex problems.

Scarborough, like nearby beaches, is a good site for observing wintering birds. Ducks, loons, grebes, and occasionally harlequin duck may be seen.

At the intersection of Rte. 1 and Rte. 207 at Oak Hill, follow Rte. 207 for 3½ miles south toward Prout's Neck. The beach and parking area are located on the left. Scarborough Beach is well used during the summer and parking may be a problem. Fee: $ .75 per car.

Crescent Beach State Park

Crescent Beach is a small fringing pocket beach. The sediments are derived from offshore glacial deposits as well as some bedrock erosion from the local headland. In the summer, there is a marked build-up of the berm, well illustrating the seasonal profile. Two factors figure in sand distribution along the stretch: transport eastward due to dry western winds and transport westward due to eastern waves. In this case, the waves have predominated, building up sand deposits on the western end of the beach and maintaining a sand-starved state in the eastern end. To the west of the sand beach, a polished stone beach extends for almost a mile, and part of this area is included in the park. Although Crescent Beach has no parabolic dunes, it does have a region of dry dune flats with a healthy dune plant population. It is also the northernmost beach in Maine which has a stand of tall wormwood.

Crescent Beach looks out to Richmond Island, which was once one of the largest trading centers on the Atlantic coast. George Richmond of Ireland established a trading post here in 1620. The post was managed by various men, including one Walter Bagnall, who not only was a crafty trader, but cheated the Indians and met his reckoning at their hand. John Winter built up the trade, and from 1633-1645 the island flourished. In 1645, Winter died, trade declined, and relations with the Indians—which were never good—worsened. Richmond Island slumped into obscurity for over 200 years. Then, one sunny day in 1855, a tenant farmer plowed up a pottery crock containing gold and silver coins dating from the 16th and 17th centuries. Apparently Walter Bagnall, knowing that his end was near, had buried all of his ill-gained wealth but was unable to leave word of its whereabouts. The treasure of Richmond Island was found without even the assistance of a map.

The island is presently uninhabited. Livestock and deer graze on the grass, harbor seals often sun on the nearby ledges, and little about the place indicates that it was once a bustling center of commerce.

Take Rte. 77 south out of South Portland to Cape Elizabeth. Follow signs for Crescent Beach State Park. Fee: $ .75 per car.

Two Lights State Park

Two Lights State Park has a dramatic view of Casco Bay and the Atlantic Ocean. Traveling due east, the next land encountered is Spain. Equally impressive is the exposure of slightly metamorphosed, limey shale which forms a steep, rocky shoreline. Ancient deposits of clay, laid down over thousands of years, formed a thick bed of shale which was then subjected to heat and pressure. The deformation left the rocks turned and twisted, and erosion has exposed them to view.

Basins along the shore form large tide pools which harbor periwinkles, starfish, limpets, sea lettuce, rockweed, and other small plants and animals. White-tailed deer, raccoon, skunk, woodchuck, and rabbit browse in the woods nearby.

Take Rte. 77 south out of South Portland to Cape Elizabeth. Follow signs for Two Lights State Park. Fee: $ .75 per car.

Portland-Freeport

Back Cove

Route 295 in Portland passes by beautiful stretches of marshland. The silhouette of a great blue heron darting for fish, even seen from a fast-moving automobile, is a treasured picture. The Back Cove area, 33 acres of tidal flats, has been preserved as a bird sanctuary within the city by the Department of Inland Fisheries and Wildlife. Migrating shorebirds bob and scamper for food; black duck, bufflehead, goldeneye and scaup winter over; and all the while the skyline of Portland grows and changes.

Traveling north on Rte. 295 through Portland, take the Forest Ave. North Exit (Rte. 100) and immediately turn onto Baxter Boulevard, which circumnavigates Back Cove. (Going south on Rte. 295, take the Baxter Boulevard Exit.) A parking lot and sheltered picnic tables are located along the northeast section of the cove. Free admission.

Gilsland Farm

Gilsland Farm, headquarters for the Maine Audubon Society, is a 70-acre area which lies along the Presumpscot River. It is the largest natural area easily accessible from Portland. An extensive trail system runs through fields, mixed hardwoods, conifers, marsh, and along the tidal estuary. The farm is a favorite spot for cross-country skiers and snowshoers, as the tracks of many shy animals can be seen in the snow. Maine Audubon provides a trail brochure as well as a self-guided tour of the headquarters, which is the largest solar-heated building in Maine. Specially designed for cold Maine weather, the solar collectors heat air rather than water (which could freeze) and the heat is stored in a large bed of crushed rock. A wood furnace backs up the solar collectors and provides auxiliary heat during long stretches of cold, cloudy weather.

Maine Audubon is active in many aspects of natural history and con-

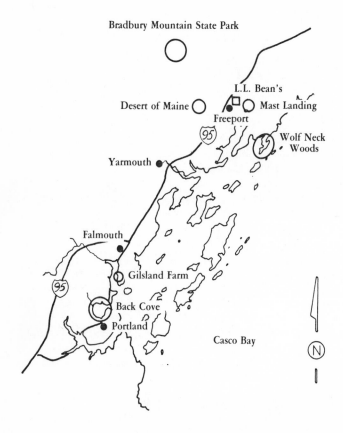

Bradbury Mountain State Park

L.L. Bean's

Desert of Maine   Mast Landing

Freeport

95

Wolf Neck
Woods

Yarmouth

Falmouth

95

Gilsland Farm

Back Cove

Portland

Casco Bay

N

Map 3   Portland—Freeport

servation of natural resources. The Society operates three nature centers, houses an extensive natural history library, and offers a variety of field trips. It also sponsors a weekend birding conference each spring and an energy conference in the fall. For more information about the activities and trips, write:

Maine Audubon Society
Gilsland Farm
Old Route 1
Falmouth, Maine 04105

From Rte. 295 in Portland, take the Falmouth Foreside Exit onto Rte. 1 and cross the Presumpscot River bridge. After 1.6 miles veer left onto a small access road and turn left at the Maine Audubon sign. Follow the dirt road to the visitor parking area and headquarters building. Free admission.

Freeport: L.L. Bean's

Although L.L. Bean's is not a "natural area," it attracts thousands of nature lovers each year. Leon L. Bean founded the enterprise in 1912, when he created a novel waterproof boot which had a rubber sole and leather uppers. He opened a showroom in 1940 and when he grew tired of answering late-night phone calls and requests, he kept the store open 24 hours a day, 365 days a year. The store retails a huge variety of sporting goods, tents, canoes, and outdoor equipment, but the outlet accounts for only 20% of the volume. Over 2 million catalogs are published each year and mail order business contributes 80% of the annual sales. The store may have lost its old-time flavor when the building was face-lifted but, to a million customers, "Bean's" is still a magic word.

From US 95, take any of the Freeport Exits to the center of Freeport. Free admission, but you may not want to leave without buying something!

Desert of Maine

The Desert of Maine is part of a large glacial outwash plain which has little vegetative cover as a result of overgrazing by sheep. The drifting sand has overtaken land and some buildings and is now advancing into the eastern wooded area. As a section is swept clear of sand and the water table is exposed, mosses and lichens are able to take hold and begin the process of revegetation. Upwind perimeter areas are being naturally reclaimed. Rainwater has soaked through the sand at varying rates, caus-

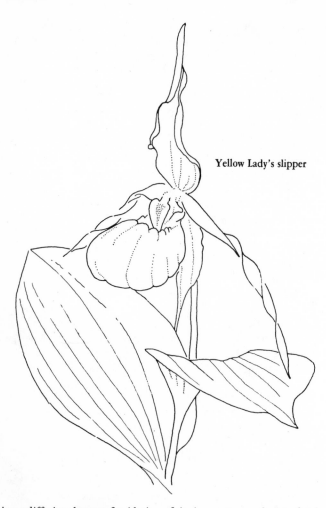

Yellow Lady's slipper

ing a differing degree of oxidation of the iron compounds. In a few loca-
tions, a variegated landscape of pinks and browns has been produced.
    From US 95, take the Desert Road Exit near Freeport and travel 2
miles west to the entrance. The Desert of Maine is managed as a
commercial enterprise. Fee: $1.50 per person.

Mast Landing
Mast Landing is a well known historical as well as natural area. Huge

pines destined to be masts for English ships were cut and dragged to the Harraseckit River. The large triangular road juncture in the center of Freeport, where Route 1 connects with Bow Street, was constructed so that teams of oxen could "turn the corner" with their loads. The Revolutionary War terminated British supply, but not before hundreds of American pines were flying the Union Jack.

The sanctuary has extensive trails which travel through fields, woods and marsh, providing a variety of habitats for birdwatchers and naturalists. Brochures to the nature trails are available at the house near the parking lot. It is an excellent public use area for hiking, picnicking, nature walks, cross-country skiing, and snowshoeing. Maine Audubon owns the 150-acre tract and runs a nature day-camp in the summer.

From Rte. 1 in Freeport, turn east onto Bow Street, just in front of Bean's. Follow the road 1 mile (it becomes Flying Point Road) and turn north at the Mast Landing sign. Take the first right turn, which is the entrance to the sanctuary and parking lot. Free admission.

Wolf Neck Woods

Wolf Neck Woods is a 200-acre state park of climax hemlock forest, mixed hardwoods, pine, rocky shore, and an osprey sanctuary. The well-developed trail system includes information panels which explain aspects of local geology, biology, and history. The park is often used by school groups and a natural history program is underway. The area is also a favorite for picnicking in the summer and cross-country skiing in the winter.

The rocks exposed along the eastern shore of Wolf Neck include amphibolite, a dark metavolcanic rock (a metamorphosed igneous rock which was produced by volcanism) and younger granites and pegmatites. Veins of light-colored quartz and wider dikes of pegmatite have clearly intruded the amphibolite, indicating the relative youth of the quartz and pegmatite. Stone walls composed of glacial till which cut through the woods are reminders of recent geology and also mark previous farmland which has now grown into pine.

The osprey nest is located in a tall, dead pine on Googins Island, just east of the neck. Ospreys have lived at Wolf Neck for over 75 years. They mate for life and return to the same nest year after year. If one pair fails to return, another pair will take over the nest. Ospreys, eagles, and other birds of prey are particularly susceptible to pesticide poisoning. The chemicals prevent proper absorption and use of calcium, producing thin, easily cracked eggs. The Wolf Neck pair—unlike most New

Osprey

England ospreys—was not strongly affected and has produced at least one chick each year. The birds return from South America in April, hatch one and occasionally two chicks in mid-May, raise the young, and migrate south in October. They are often seen fishing before and during low tide (when fish are concentrated in channels), and are commonly called "fish hawks." The birds become disturbed if visitors cross onto the island at low tide, and the area has been set aside as a sanctuary.

From Rte. 1 in Freeport, turn east onto Bow Street. Follow the road 2.3 miles (past Mast Landing) and turn right at the sign for the park. Continue 2.1 miles and turn left onto the park entrance road. Fee: $ .75 per car.

Bradbury Mountain

Bradbury Mountain is a large granite intrusion which has resisted erosion and stands 500 feet above the surrounding countryside. Two easy trails lead from the picnic area through mixed hardwoods and large hemlock to the summit, where there is a fine view of Casco Bay and the White Mountains. The summit is also a perfect spot to watch migrating hawks in the fall. A small herd of deer and some moose winter in the area, as well as various smaller animals such as raccoon and porcupine. Bradbury Mountain State Park encompasses 2 acres, although most of the land is thickly wooded and without trails.

Take the Bradbury Mountain Exit off of US 95 at Freeport. Continue 6 miles to the park entrance. Fee: $ .75 per car.

Freeport-Bath

Maquoit Bay

Maquoit Bay is a shallow, warm-water bay that is rich in clams, mussels, and quahogs, and consequently is also rich in migrating shore birds and waterfowl. As with most good birding sites, regular visits prove more fruitful than "one big day of birding." A single trip to Maquoit Bay in September may turn up many species, but visits each Sunday afternoon provide a sense of the season as well as a chance to see a wide range of migrants—including uncommon species. Simply, the more one watches, the more one sees.

From the center of Brunswick, follow Rte. 24 to Bowdoin College. Veer right when Rte. 24 turns left, continue for 1 mile on Main Street, and bear right again onto Maquoit Road. Go almost 2 miles to the head of the bay. Free.

Bowdoin Pines

Bowdoin Pines are the prize of Brunswick and Bowdoin College. The stand of cathedral white pines is actually only 105 years old, much younger than the college which was chartered in 1794. The site was probably cleared for farmland and later abandoned. White pines took over and in the rich soil grew into large, healthy trees. If natural succession is allowed to continue hardwoods will eventually replace the pines.

From the center of Brunswick, follow Rte. 24 north around Bowdoin College. The pine stand is located just north of the turn-off for Rte. 123. Free.

Topsham

Over 34 mines and quarries are located in the Topsham area. Fisher Quarry, the largest, mined 17,000 tons of feldspar per year at the height of production. Although the mines are not as rich in gemstones as Mt.

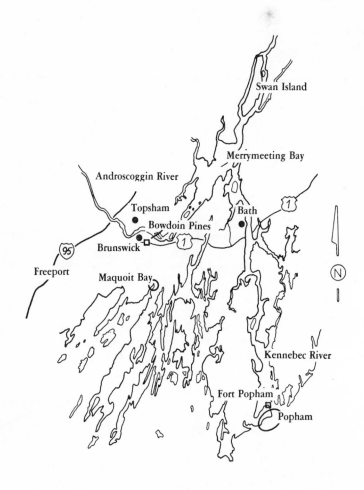

Map 4   Freeport-Bath

Mica in Auburn or Black Mountain Mica Mines in Rumford, they have produced specimens of beryl, garnet, tourmaline, columbite, biotite and muscovite.

All of these minerals are found in pegmatite, a course-grained rock composed chiefly of quartz, feldspar and mica. Pockets of pegmatite are found in granite. Slower cooling of molten rock in these pockets allowed larger growth of crystals, which range from a few inches to many feet. Pegmatites are mined primarily for potash feldspar, used in fine porcelain and scouring powder, and sometimes include gemstones.

A comprehensive booklet available for $ .50 (plus tax) lists and describes many public rock collecting locations. *Maine Pegmatite Mines and Prospects and Associated Minerals* by John R. Rand (1957) is available from:

Maine Department of Economic Development
Augusta, Maine 04333

Popham Beach

Popham Beach is one of the most complex beach systems in Maine. The area from the Morse River to Fort Popham includes 3 beaches, a spit, 2 tombolos, cuspate forelands, and large stabilized parabolic dunes in a pitch pine forest. The eastern half of Hunnewell Beach and Coast Guard Beach are developed, but western Hunnewell and what is generally referred to as Popham Beach are owned and managed by the state. The features of the state-owned area are described in this section. Because the Popham system is extremely unstable, it is an excellent site for observing beach features.

A small area of semi-vegetated dunes surrounds the Popham parking area. These parabolic dunes were active 30-40 years ago and were formed by strong northwest winds. To the west of the parking lot, dunes have been stabilized by a climax pitch pine forest. The forest includes several inland forest species and a soil layer and is therefore the least fragile part of the system. A rear dune bridge can be seen northwest of the pine forest. To the south of the parking lot, a large southwest-facing frontal dune ridge has formed as a result of strong southwest winds. Popham Beach and Seawall Beach form a double spit at the mouth of the Morse River. The eastern spit formed in the 1940s as a result of meandering of the Morse River, and the spit has since protected an area of sand flats allowing salt marsh grass, *Spartina*, to become established.

Fox Island and Wood Island are erosion-resistant granite and schist outcrops. Intertidal tombolos and cuspate forelands have formed in the

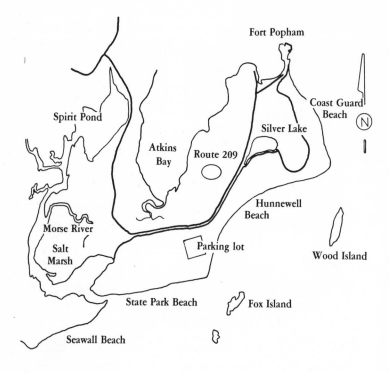

Popham Beach

lee of the islands. Two large offshore bars to either side of Fox Island protect the beach and supply sand to the landward berm and dunes. The bars formed in 1975 and are migrating toward the shore. This recent protection has allowed the berm west of the cuspate foreland to begin accreting and it is being colonized by American beachgrass, dusty miller, and other berm pioneers. It is unusual that two frontal dune ridges, one behind the other, are actively growing behind the berm.

Popham, unlike most Maine beaches which derive sand from outwash plains, is supplied with sand by the Kennebec River. Currents produced by the Kennebec River, the Morse River and tides set up a complex cycle of sand deposition and erosion. In recent years, dramatic erosion of the beach bordering private property has triggered concerning the construction of seawalls.

Fort Popham, at the northern tip of the beach system, was built in 1861 to protect the Kennebec River. Near this site, Sir John Popham and a group of colonists landed their ship on a warm August day in 1607. But ill fate badgered the settlement. Insufficient supplies, a severe winter, a devastating fire in the store house, and the death of Sir John Popham overwhelmed the colonists, and they sailed for England the following summer.

From Rte. 1 in Bath, take Rte. 207 toward Phippsburg. Continue 12 miles, following signs for the park. Fee: $1.50 per car.

Merrymeeting Bay

Merrymeeting Bay is the largest tidal bay north of the Chesapeake and is therefore the northernmost U.S. stopover on the Atlantic Flyway. Each spring and fall migrating Canada goose, black duck, green-winged teal, blue-winged teal, common goldeneye, American wigeon, pintail, and other birds rest and feed in the marsh. In the spring, it has Maine's largest concentration of Canada geese.

Maine is the only state north of Maryland where eagles nest in any numbers along the coast. Although 10-20 pair formerly nested in Merrymeeting Bay, there are now two known pair and one immature. Eggs from the area have shown exceptionally high concentrations of DDT, which prevents the formation of a strong shell, and eagles are not able to maintain a steady population. The Department of Inland Fish and Wildlife initiated a program of egg transplants in an attempt to bolster the declining numbers. Healthy eggs from nests in the mid-west, where the population is stable, were substituted for cracked eggs in the Merrymeeting Bay nests. The immature eagle which resides in the area hatched from a Wisconsin egg. But not all of the transplants were successful, and no one can say for certain when and if bald eagles will make a come-back in Maine.

Merrymeeting Bay provides nesting sites for black duck, ring-necked duck, blue-winged teal, green-winged teal, and mergansers. Common snipe, bittern, pied-billed grebe, greater yellowlegs, lesser yellowlegs, herring gull, and great black-backed gull are commonly seen. Beaver, otter, muskrat, and raccoon inhabit the area. The bay also provides habitat for a substantial smelt, alewife, and striped bass fishery. The Kennebec River in the past supported a large run of Atlantic salmon, but dams and pollution destroyed most spawning grounds. However,

Canada Goose

the salmon are beginning to run again as stricter environmental laws are improving the condition of the river.

Merrymeeting Bay is formed by the confluence of six rivers: the Androscoggin, Kennebec, Muddy, Cathance, Abagaddasset, and Eastern. It was a traditional summering place for Indians who relied on the abundant fish, fowl, and game. Local history holds that Arnold and his men stopped at Swan Island for a large feast with the Indians before striking out on their devastating trek to Quebec.

Although the bay includes 4500 acres, much of the surrounding land is privately owned. Public roads run along the bay at two points. 1) From Rte. 201 in Topsham, turn east on Rte. 24 for ½ mile. Turn right onto the road which runs along the Androscoggin River. Travel 4½ miles and take another right to Pleasant Point, which overlooks the southern half of the bay. 2) Stay on Rte. 24 through Bowdoinham, but fork right when Rte. 24 turns north to Richmond. 1.3 miles past the town, the road will cross over the Abagadasset, offering a second view. Free.

Swan Island

The Steve Powell Wildlife Management Area, better known as Swan Island, lies in the northern stretch of Merrymeeting Bay. Swan Island sustains a variety of wildlife, including a large population of deer. The area is available in the summer months of day use and overnight camping. Although visitors are generally restricted from the southwest half of the island, a half-hour bus tour given by the Department of Inland Fisheries and Wildlife highlights special parts of the island, including the eagle nest.

For information, reservations, and fee schedule, write Wildlife Division, Department of Inland Fisheries and Wildlife, 284 State Street, Augusta, Maine 04333. The I.F.W. provides ferry service from Richmond.

Bath-Damariscotta

Robert P.T. Coffin Wildflower Reservation

Robert P. Tristam Coffin wrote *Kennebec, Cradle of America, Salt Water Farm, Christmas in Maine*, and many other books about early Maine life. The works reflect his deep pride in the state, and it is appropriate that the sanctuary on the Kennebec River is named in his honor. The reservation is a secluded, quiet area owned by the New England Wildflower Society and it is used primarily for the study of plant life and for birdwatching.

The 175-acre tract is divided into two pieces, one parcel east of Route 128 and the second bordering Merrymeeting Bay. A maintained trail running through each section traverses mixed forest of hemlock, pine, and hardwoods. The reservation is particularly beautiful in the spring and early summer, when woodland wildflowers carpet the forest floor. In the spring and fall, migrating shorebirds, ducks, and geese can be seen from the western trail which overlooks the bay.

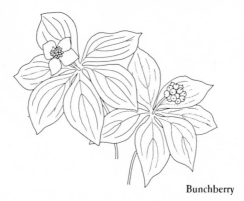

Bunchberry

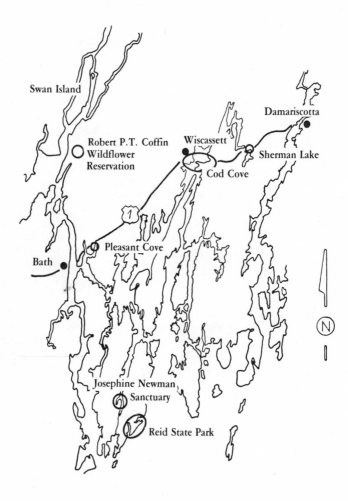

Map 5   Bath-Damariscotta

From US 1 in Woolwich, turn north onto Rte. 127 for 1.8 miles, Turn left onto Rte. 128, proceed 4.3 miles, and park at the white church. Walk 20 yards farther along the road and turn right onto an old dirt road to explore the first area. The second area is ½ mile beyond the church. Park at the turn-off for Chop Point and walk 20 yards along the left hand side of the road. The trail begins at the Coffin Wildflower Reservation sign. Free admission.

Pleasant Cove

Pleasant Cove is a small, scenic natural resource protection area. Wild rice and bullrushes attract a variety of shorebirds during migration. The small body of open water on the west side of Route 1 is a good spot to see transient ring-necked duck, wood duck, Canada goose, and other waterfowl. Pleasant Cove is not a major birding area by any means. It is what the name says: a pleasant place to stop for a few minutes to watch ducks dabble for food, to feel the breeze off the water, to listen to the grasses swish and sway.

From the Bath Bridge, go north on Rte. 1 for 1 mile and pull off on Old Rte. 1 to view the cove. Free.

Josephine Newman Sanctuary

Josephine Newman was a tiny, spry woman. For many years she lived alone in her old farmhouse, snowshoeing to the well for water, writing by lamplight instead of electricity, studying mosses and lichens with a well worn microscope. Her careful work added a new species, *Pseudiscothecium*, to the list of mosses in Maine and she received a bronze medal at the Boston Flower Show for her exhibit of native mosses.

Mrs. Newman gave 400 acres near Robin Hood Cover to the Maine Audubon Society so that the land she loved could be protected and preserved. The sanctuary has a good cross-section of coastal habitats, including a meadow, pine grove, cattail pond, high arid knoll, several small cliffs, and ledges which overlook Robin Hood Cove. Five miles of trails are maintained for birdwatching, snowshoeing and winter ecology, and general nature exploration. The exposed rocks are metasedimentary (primarily schist and phyllite) and metavolcanic, meaning that the original sedimentary and volcanic rocks were metamorphosed during the Acadian mountain-building period 390 million years ago. Mrs. Newman's house is no longer standing, but Merrymeeting Audubon Society has planted an herb garden in the old foundation, honoring the woman who cared so greatly for the small things of the earth.

North of the Bath Bridge, turn off US 1 and onto Rte. 127 toward Reid State Park. Continue for 8.8 miles. Just after the Georgetown bridge, turn right on the access road marked by the Maine Audubon sign, and park at the end of the dirt road. Free.

Reid State Park

Reid State Park includes two beaches, a rocky shore, and a large marsh. It is an excellent area for observing wintering ducks, migrating shorebirds, marsh birds and occasional harbor seals. The park contains the most northern large dune field and is biologically important as the northernmost beach heather habitat in the state. It is also the northernmost potential nesting habitat for least terns and piping plover, although heavy recreational use and a nonaccreting berm presently prevent the birds from nesting.

Mile Beach, the long straight beach which stretches between Griffith's Head and Todd's Head, is a closed barrier which has formed at the mouth of the subsurface rock embayment. (Because it is located at the bay's mouth, the beach receives waves directly and is therefore a straight feature. If the beach were at the head of Sheepscot Bay, it would be rounded as a result of the refraction of waves.) Onshore winds have moved sand up the beach face and formed a large frontal dune ridge. The ridge's backslope extends well into the rear dune field. Geologists hypothesize that as the ridge migrates landward to keep pace with the rising sea level, the dune field is not able to move as quickly, resulting in a very narrow field. The narrowness of this area in conjunction with high energy waves which splash salt spray landward prevent the growth of pitch pine on the dunes. The large marsh which lies to the rear of Mile Beach was once a freshwater pond but now connects with the sea through a man-made inlet north of Griffith Head.

Half Mile Beach, to the west of Todds Head, is an open barrier spit which protects a large salt marsh. The Little River, a tidal reentrant, drains west of the spit. Northwest winds carry sand from the Little River shore to the backdunes of Half Mile Beach, where several small parabolic dunes have formed. As the river channel has migrated landward in response to sea level rise, so has the dune area moved inland. Two shoreline ridges which once marked the edge of the river are now incorporated into the dune field. Half Mile Beach is at the down-drift end of the Reid system and is composed of smaller sand particles than Mile Beach, as light sediments are carried further than heavy ones. Both beaches at Reid have a high percentage of schist and feldspar fragments, indicating erosion from the local schist and gneiss bedrock, rather than long-distance transport via the Kennebec River. The "young" sand at Reid has been moved only a short distance from nearby headlands and glacial deposits.

North of the Bath Bridge, turn off US 1 and onto Rte. 127. Drive 10 miles and turn right at the state park sign. Continue 2 miles to park entrance. Fee: $1.50 per car.

Cod Cove

Cod Cove is a high yield area for marine sandworms and bloodworms. The worms are dug, sold to dealers, and shipped throughout the country where they are a popular bait of sport fishermen. Many good worming flats are located near Wiscasset, making it the center of the two-million-dollar industry. Wormers can be seen on the mudflats, winter and summer, and many of them work both tides even through the bitterest weather.

Cod Cove is ½ mile east of Wiscasset on US 1. Free.

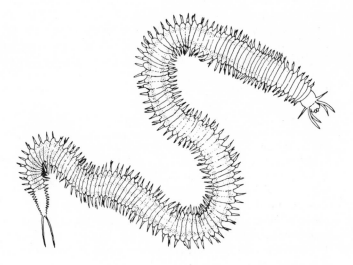

Marine worm

Sherman Lake

The Sherman Lake rest area in Newcastle overlooks Sherman Lake and the adjoining freshwater marsh. The moderate-sized lake was created when the highway was constructed. It is a good site for observing freshwater ducks. Marsh wren, bobolink, and red-winged blackbird nest in the cattails. Like Pleasant Cove near Bath, Sherman Lake is not an outstanding area in that is has no unusual plant or animal species. What it does provide, however, is a beautiful place to stop, eat lunch, and stretch one's legs and such places are valuable for just that reason.

From the Wiscasset Bridge, drive 3.2 miles northeast on US 1.
Free.

Damariscotta-Camden

Salt Bay

Salt Bay is a large, shallow area with exposed flats at low tide. It serves as a flyway stopover for migrating birds and a nesting spot for a pair of osprey. The large nest is located in an electrical pole on the island in the middle of the lake. Ospreys will build a nest in any sturdy, convenient platform, including poles, stationary channel markers, and trees.

The Damariscotta alewife run, which accounts for 29 percent of the catch in Maine, passes through the bay. The alewife is an anadromous fish which, like the Atlantic salmon, lives in the ocean but ascends rivers to spawn. The Damariscotta River did not originally support an alewife run, as few fish could navigate the 50-foot falls en route to Damariscotta Lake, but in 1806 a rock fishway was built and the area was stocked. Alewives are used primarily as lobster bait.

Going north on US 1, take the Damariscotta Exit and immediately turn north onto Rte. 213 toward Damariscotta Mills. Continue ½ mile and pull off by the side of the road to view the tidal flats and osprey nest. Free.

Colonial Pemaquid

Colonial Pemaquid is the site of an extensive archaeological dig. Scientists have excavated foundations of 14 homes built in the 1500s and 1600s, the era of early exploration and colonization. Fort William Henry was first built here around 1630 as a defense against pirates. The current building is a replica of the third of four forts which protected the Damariscotta settlements. Adjacent to the site is a privately managed museum.

From Damariscotta, take Rte. 129 south, bearing left after 4 miles onto Rte. 130. Continue 9 miles and turn right at the sign for the town of Pemaquid Beach. In town, follow the sign for Colonial Pemaquid. Fee: $ .25 per person for Fort William Henry.

to Camden

90

Glen Cove

Rockland
Marsh

90

Rockland

Waldoboro

1

1

Thomaston

Salt Bay

1

Hospital Cove

Weskeag Marsh

Damariscotta

Birch Point
Beach

Hocomock
Nature Trail

Friendship

Hog Island

Tenants Harbor

Port Clyde

N

Rachael Carson
Salt Pond Preserve

Pemaquid Point

Map 6   Damariscotta-Camden

Pemaquid Beach

Pemaquid Beach is an excellent illustration of a closed pocket barrier beach. Its sand was transported from nearby glacial deposits and includes flecks of eroded minerals like biotite, a dark-colored mica. The minerals are well sorted, as fine, white, quartz-rich sand is found on the berm, while dark mineral sediments lie along the lower beach face. Pemaquid has a "low sand budget," which means that in winter, when the sand is eroded from the berm and deposited offshore, an underlying surface of stones and pebbles is revealed. Tree stumps and marsh peat are also exposed, indicating that the beach has moved inland in response to the rising sea level.

During the severe winter storms of 1978, the edge of the dune field was eroded and the remaining field washed over by waves. Several inches of sand were deposited on the dunes and in the marsh. In effect, the beach moved inland and this move will counter-balance many years of gradual sea level rise.

Seaweed which is raked up the beach by the maintenance staff fertilizes the frontal dune ridge and allows a variety of dune and non-dune plant species. American beachgrass, the predominant cover in southern beaches and the only true dune plant which grows on beaches north of Pemaquid, does not successfully compete with these other species.

Follow above directions to the town of Pemaquid Beach. Once in town, turn left toward Pemaquid Point and drive 0.2 miles to the beach. Fee: $ .65 per person.

Pemaquid Point

Pemaquid Point overlooks Muscungus Bay. Visitors are immediately struck by the vast and beautiful exposure of rocks. These formations originated millions of years ago as ocean currents, heavily laden with mud, deposited thick layers of sediments on the ocean floor. The mud layers formed graywacke, a dark sedimentary rock. Thin layers of limestone—the remains of minute radiolarian protozoa—were intermittently laid down with the mud, producing light and dark banding. When movement of the tectonic plates folded the coastal margins, the graywacke was metamorphosed but it retained the banded appearance. The upturned exposure is therefore "meta"wacke with thinly bedded limey quartzite layers. Erosion by waves has left the rocks smooth and beautifully sculpted.

Common eider often raft in the winter off Pemaquid Point and upon occasion 600-700 ducks have been reported. Kresge Point, just south of Pemaquid, is a stop-over on the migration route of the monarch but-

Eider ducks, male and female.

terfly. Monarchs avoid the killing cold of northern winters by flying south, where they winter in the Sierra Madre Mountains of Mexico.

Going north on US 1, take the Damariscotta Exit and follow Rte. 129 for 4 miles. Veer left on Rte. 130 for 11½ miles. Fee: $ .25 per person. Fisherman's Museum at site: $ .50 per person.

Rachael Carson Salt Pond Preserve

The Rachael Carson Salt Pond Preserve is located in a small cove near New Harbor where Rachael Carson studied marine life. The large pool created at low tide provided much material for her book, *The Edge of the Sea*, and is still an excellent spot for investigating marine ecology.

The area also has several interesting geological sites. About 55 yards north of the Rachael Carson monument along the high tide line an exposed sill illustrates "boudinage" (French for sausage). Sausage-like shapes were created as molten magma forced its way between layers of the dark gray gneiss. Later, both the gneiss and pegmatite intrusions were folded during the Acadian mountain building period and fresh magma invaded the area, producing light-colored granite bodies. The granite outcrop several yards south of the sill indicates still further deformation, for the granite has been broken and recemented by thick quartz veins.

The granite and gneiss demonstrate differential erosion. Small grains weather more easily than large ones, and the finer grained gneiss erodes much more quickly than the coarser grained granite. Gneiss which has been folded and upturned is especially susceptible to erosion, as water and ice work between layers and fragment the ledges.

Guide·Book to Geologic and Beach Features of the Rachael Carson Salt Pond Area, by Vandall King and Bruce Nelson, describes these and other features along a short walking tour of the cove. The booklet (Sea Grant Information Leaflet #12) is available at no cost from:

Ira C. Darling Center
Walpole, Maine 04573.

From Damariscotta, follow Rte. 129 for 4 miles, veer left onto Rte. 130 for 9 miles, and turn left at the sign for New Harbor. Travel 1.2 miles and, just past the town, pull off onto the scenic view area along the road. The Rachael Carson Memorial is a small plaque set in a granite boulder near the southern end of the lookout. Free.

Hocomock Nature Trail

The Hocomock Nature Trail is a short, educational walk through field, forest, and shoreline. The unpretentious trail guide is full of nature lore—bird calls, tree identification, animal habits—and is suited to children as well as adults. The trail runs near Hog Island, also known as Todd Wildlife Sanctuary, where National Audubon Society operates a summer nature study program. Two-week coastal ecology workshops for adults are held throughout the summer. Further information about these programs can be obtained at the house near the beginning of the trail or by writing:

Environmental Information and Education Department
National Audubon Society
950 Third Avenue
New York, New York 10022

From Rte. 1 in Waldoboro, take Rte. 32 south 7½ miles. Turn left onto Keene Neck Road at the sign for the Audubon Camp. Follow the road 2 miles until it ends and park in the visitor lot. Walk between the barn and house to the beginning of the trail, where a small box contains trail guides. Free.

Birch Point Beach

Birch Point Beach, also known as Lucia Beach, is owned by the state but has not yet been developed as a park. Facilities may be missing, but interesting natural history is not. Birch Point is a fringing pocket beach with a small freshwater marsh squeezed between the upper rocky ridge and the upland. Rocky headlands composed of granite with flakes of biotite (black mica) and biotite-muscovite (black and light colored mica) protect each end of the area. Eider and guillemots can be seen from Otter Point, the southern headland, and the point also offers an excellent view of the Muscle Ridge Islands.

One foggy night toward the end of the Revolutionary War, a British sloop-of-war, *Albany*, wrecked on the Northern Triangles beyond the Muscle Ridges. The soldiers abandoned ship, climbed into an open boat, and soon became lost in the dense fog. They missed the mainland altogether, heading instead toward the open ocean. Only by chance did they come upon Matinicus Island, a solitary outpost, where they were taken in and cared for.

From the center of South Thomaston, continue east when Rte. 73 turns north. Travel 1.3 miles and turn right just past airport landing lights. Go 0.8 miles and fork left through old gates onto a poor dirt road. Drive 0.4 miles to the parking lot. Free.

Rockland Bog

The 650-acre Rockland Bog and 5500 acres surrounding it are collectively the Oyster River Bog. The area supports a wide variety of plant, mammal, and bird life which is well described in *A Special Place: The Story of the Oyster River Bog*, published by the Oyster River Bog Study Group. Although the area is privately owned and is therefore not open to the public, the study group has developed an excellent slide show and makes arrangements for educational visits. Inquiries and requests should be addressed to:

James Tucker
Mill Road
West Rockport, Maine 04856

Shorebird and Waterfowl Areas

There are a number of good sites in this region for observing migrating shorebirds and wintering ducks:

Friendship Harbor: Wintering birds, occasionally dovekies after a storm. From US 1 in Warren, take Rte. 97 10 miles to Friendship.

Port Clyde Harbor: Wintering ducks. Take Rte. 131 13 miles south from Thomaston.

Tenants Harbor: Wintering ducks. Take Rte. 131 9 miles south from Thomaston.

Burreed

Hospital Cove in Thomaston: Extensive mudflats for migrating shorebirds. Turn right off US 1 just before the big cove north of the town.

Weskeag Marsh in South Thomaston: All types of waterfowl, including ducks, geese, and shorebirds. This wildlife area is managed by the Department of Inland Fisheries and Wildlife. From US 1 in Rockland, take Rte. 73 4 miles south to the bridge in South Thomaston, which overlooks the marsh.

Glen Cove: Migrating shorebirds and wintering ducks. From US 1 just north of Rockland, pull off at the Department of Transportation Rest Stop at Glen Cove.

Camden-Ellsworth

Camden Hills

All I could see from where I stood
Was three long mountains and a wood;
I turned and looked another way,
And saw three islands in a bay.
So with my eyes I traced a line
Of the horizon, thin and fine,
Straight around til I was come
Back to where I started from;
And all I saw from where I stood
Was three long mountains and a wood.

Who could better describe the view from the summit of Mt. Battie than Edna St. Vincent Millay, who lived in Camden and loved to climb in the Camden Hills? This first stanza is from "Renascence," which she wrote at the age of eighteen. The poem brought her recognition and a patron, and for many years she lived far from her native state. Her poems, though, always reflected her longing for the Maine coast.

Visitors can follow Edna St. Vincent Millay's footsteps to the top of Mt. Battie. Other trails lead to Bald Rock Mountain, Cameron Mountain, and Mt. Megunticook (the second highest point along the Atlantic seaboard). A map and trail description, available at the park entrance, indicate difficulty and aid hikers, cross-country skiers, snowshoers, and birdwatchers in choosing an appropriate trip. Mt. Battie is an excellent point for watching the annual fall migration of hawks.

Main Entrance to Camden Hills State Park is just north of Camden on US Rte. 1. Fee: $ .75 per car.

Penobscot and Union Rivers

Salmon is an anadromous fish. It lives in the ocean but returns to fresh water, usually the site where it hatched, to spawn. Atlantic salmon was

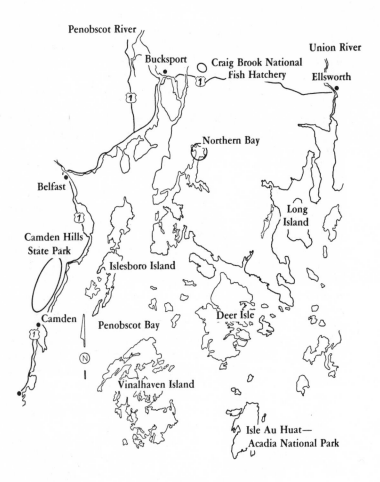

Map 7   Camden-Ellsworth

so common in colonial days that farmers used the fish as fertilizer. Although pollution, overfishing, and disruption of habitat eliminated the species from many areas, Maine is still the only state on the East coast which has self-sustaining runs of salmon, and the Penobscot and Union Rivers have been reestablished through pollution control and stocking.

Fresh run or "bright" fish enter Maine's rivers from spring through October. Small rivers usually have one peak run period from May through July. Salmon spawn in October or early November, laying eggs in small pits scooped out of a gravel bottom. A fast current is necessary to keep the eggs well oxygenated. Unlike Pacific salmon, Atlantic salmon do not always die after spawning. The "kelts" or post-spawners return immediately to the ocean or wait until spring to make the trip. Eggs hatch in March. Young salmon remain in fresh water for two or three years before turning toward the ocean.

Atlantic salmon off of Nova Scotia, Newfoundland, Labrador, and Greenland. Only adults which have spent one winter at sea make the 2000 mile trip to Greenland, where excellent feeding grounds also attract European salmon. Fisheries biologists calculate that fish migrating from Maine waters average more than 10-15 miles per day in the long journey to and from this wintering area.

The Sheepscot, Narraguagus, Pleasant, Machias, East Machias and Dennys Rivers also have fishable populations of Atlantic salmon. Salmon are presently returning to other rivers, like the Kennebec, as fish ladders are restored and the water quality improves.

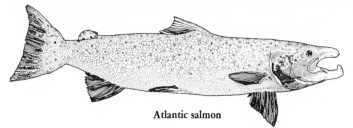

Atlantic salmon

Craig Brook National Fish Hatchery
Craig Brook Hatchery produces Atlantic salmon smolt (2 year old fish) for stocking the Penobscot and Union Rivers. Because of the danger of transmitting fish disease, the hatchery is no longer open to the public. However, a visitor center houses exhibits which describe the life history

of Atlantic salmon and hatchery techniques. A booklet available from the main office describes both the "raceway" (main section of the hatchery) and a 1.6 mile nature trail which runs through nearby woods. A picnic and swimming area are also part of the facility.

Three miles east of Orland on US 1, turn north at sign for Craig Brook National Fish Hatchery. Free.

Stanwood Homestead Museum and Sanctuary

The Stanwood Homestead Museum and Bird Sanctuary is too often overlooked by travelers en route to Acadia. The Homestead preserves the life and times of Cordelia Stanwood, a noted ornithologist who lived during the era of sea captains and coasting schooners. The natural history museum has a fine collection of eggs, nests, and stuffed birds, including owls, hawks, sea birds, ducks, and perching birds. The sanctuary, where Cordelia Stanwood observed and studied birds, protects over 100 species. The sanctuary also serves as a wild animal hospital. Injured animals are cared for and, if at all possible, are released at the point where they were discovered. For those whose interests are interdisciplinary, the Stanwood Homestead Museum and Bird Sanctuary is the perfect stop, for it combines human history, natural history, and quiet recreation in a peaceful setting.

The Museum is on Rte. 3 (the Bar Harbor Road) just east of Ellsworth. Free. See page 164 for location.

Mount Desert Island

Acadia National Park on Mt. Desert Island is one of the most beautiful and popular national parks in the country. When Samuel de Champlain charted this coast in 1604, he called it "Isle de Monts Desert," or "island of barren mountains," referring to the exposed granite outcrops. The name has since been shortened to Mt. Desert (pronounced des sert') Island. The geology, birdlife, forest ecology, and general natural history of the area are well documented. Rather than duplicating available material, following is a summary of natural history "hot spots" which are keyed to the free map available at the visitor center in Hulls Cove. Further information concerning programs, camping, and natural history guides is available at the center or by writing:

Superintendent
Acadia National Park
Hulls Cove, Maine 04644

Naturalist Programs

The schedule of nature programs at Acadia is long and varied. Typical offerings include:

Cadillac Summit Walk
Between Forest and Sea (intertidal zone)
Acadia Mountain Hike
Jordan Stream Walk
Witch Hole Pond Walk
Geology Hike
Discovery Walk
"Once Upon A Tree"
Night Prowl
Illustrated programs at Seawall Campground Amphitheater
Cruises of Frenchman Bay, Somes Sound, and nearby islands

The programs last from one to three hours and range from easy walking to moderate hiking. A full list is available at the Hulls Cove Visitor

Map 8   Mount Desert Island

Center. Some programs are by reservation only and there is a charge for cruises, so it is best to check at the main desk.

Geology

Mt. Desert is an excellent area to view geological features because so much of the island is exposed.

U-shaped valleys: The Tarn (south of Sieur de Monts Spring), Bubble Pond, Long Pond and Somes Sound.

Moraines: Jordan Pond and Long Pond are valleys with the southern end blocked by glacial moraines.

Kettle Ponds: The Bowl and Half Moon (small pond near Break Neck Ponds).

Erratics: South Bubble, South Ridge of Cadillac Mountain, rocky ledges of Otter Point, and the Bar Harbor Shore path.

Stoss and Ice topography: The Beehive, North and South Bubbles, Jordan Cliffs, Penobscot Mountain (above Jordan Pond), Eagle Cliff (above Valley Cove on St. Sauveur Mountain) and at Beech and Canada Cliffs (along the southwest corner of Echo Lake)

Birding Sites

Mt. Desert offers a variety of woodland, marsh, pond, rocky shore, and sand beach habitat to suit any birdwatching interest. Following are several particularly good sites.

Ocean Drive (from Sand Beach to Otter Cliffs): Guillemots, terns, and gulls in the summer; migrating waterfowl; wintering ducks.

Witch Hole Loop: Excellent warbler habitat in the post-fire vegetation; small ponds attract teal, ring-necked duck, bufflehead, black duck.

Tombolo between Bar Harbor and Bar Island: Great numbers of wintering ducks, especially scaup and oldsquaw; also loons and grebes.

Summit of Cadillac: Good vantage point for migratory birds, including pine grosbeak, snow bunting, hawks; snowy owl occasionally seen.

Bass Harbor Marsh and Pretty Marsh: Wading birds, migrating shorebirds.

Mount Desert Narrows: Migrating shorebirds and waterfowl, wintering ducks; especially good for early spring Canada goose.

Botanical Places of Special Interest

Bog ecology and vegetation: Big Heath.

159

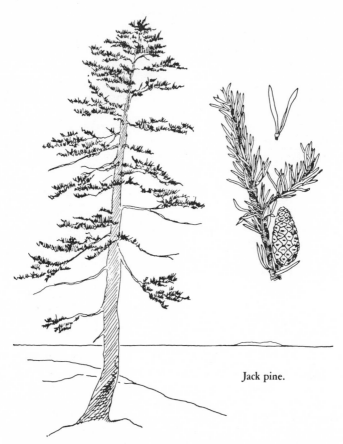

Jack pine.

Alpine vegetation: Several alpine species grow on the summits of Cadillac and Penobscot Mountains. Alpine plants are similar and sometimes include arctic and bog plants, as all three areas impose severe conditions on vegetation—poor nutrients and little usable water. Black crowberry (arctic-alpine), mountain sandwort (alpine), labrador tea (arctic-alpine-bog), and three-toothed cinquefoil (arctic-alpine-Maine coast lowland) can be seen.

Jack pines: Jack pine is uncommon in Maine but grows in several healthy stands on Mount Desert and Schoodic Peninsula. This tree is distinguished by 3/4 to 1½-inch long needles which grow in clusters of two. Pitch pine; which grows in similar habitat and is much more common, has needles 1½ to 3½-inches long, and these are born in clusters of three. Jack pines can be seen on the South Ridge Trail of Cadillac, along Route 3 just south of Huguenot Head, and on the summit of Norumbega Mountain.

Garden of native wildflowers: The Wild Gardens of Acadia are located at Sieur de Monts Spring.

Sand Beach

Sand Beach is significant for several reasons. 30-40% (by weight) of the sand is composed of carbonate, or shell fragments. No other sandy beach in Maine has such a high percentage of biogenic as opposed to glacial material. Also, no beach north of Pemaquid has as much sand per yard of beach. Glacial deposits available for beach formation are scant Downeast, and the carbonate content greatly boosts the total volume.

Sand Beach is a pocket barrier which is partly closed in the summer and open at other times of the year. This very unusual geomorphic form results from summer berm accretion and the abundance of sand in the system. The area also has a high percentage of potassium feldspar grains, giving the sand a pinkish color.

Although Sand Beach does not have dunes, it is the only beach north of Pemaquid with an aeolian flat. Healthy American beachgrass forms the largest stand in many miles.

For Further Reading:

A.M.C. Trail Guide to Mount Desert Island and Acadia National Park. (Appalachian Mountain Club, 1975)

Checklist of the Birds of Acadia National Park by Paul Favour, amended by William Townsend (Acadia National Park, 1974)

Field Guide to Acadia National Park Maine by Russell D. Butcher (Reader's Digest Press, 1977)

The Geology of Acadia National Park by Carleton A. Chapman (The Chatham Press, Inc., 1970)

A Guide to Acadia National Park by Grant W. Sharpe (Golden Press, 1968)

101 Wildflowers of Acadia National Park by Grant and Wenonah Sharpe (University of Washington Press, 1970)

Ellsworth-Cherryfield

Northern Bay and Hog Bay

Northern Bay and Hog Bay are primarily of interest to birdwatchers. Northern Bay is a shallow, muddy bay and wetlands area covering 1000 acres. It provides excellent feeding grounds for migrating ducks, geese, and shorebirds. These species can also be seen in Hog Bay, north of Route 1. Although as a species eagles are declining, the more remote regions Downeast—like Hog Bay, Machias, and Calais—are attractive nesting sites and draw a higher percentage of birds than sites in southern Maine. In this way, a small irony takes place: an endangered species can be commonly seen. Such is the case at Hog Bay, where bald eagles and ospreys both soar overhead.

To Northern Bay: From US 1 in Orland, take Rte. 175 south 11 miles to a picnic pull-off which overlooks the bay. To Hog Bay: From US 1 in Sullivan, follow Rte. 200 north 3.5 miles to East Franklin. Take the first left onto a dirt road and drive 1.6 miles, where the bay can be seen from the road. Free.

The Whaleback

The Whaleback is an outstanding example of an esker with outwash plains on both sides and boulder fields nearby. The esker is apparently part of a similar formation, the Horseback, which is located 7 miles to the northwest. Both eskers run from southeast to northwest, parallel to the direction of glacial retreat. Silsby Plain, a glacial outwash plain situated between the two eskers, is possibly a delta of the glacial river.

Route 9 runs along the top of the Whaleback. Road cuts reveal the sandy nature of the esker, but weathering has erased the fine layering of sand and pebbles. Gravel pits in the area show clear cross-bedding and layering characteristic of water-borne sediments.

Follow Rte. 9 one mile east of Aurora. The Whaleback underlies the road for 2.5 miles. Free.

Horseback

Silsby Plain

Whaleback

9

9

Deblois
Barrens

Great Heath

Rt. 193

Schoodic Lake

1

Hog Bay

1

Cherryfield

Ellsworth

1

1

Stanwood Homestead Museum
and Bird Sanctuary

3

Frenchman
Bay

1

Bar Harbor

Mt. Desert
Island

3

3

Schoodic Point

N

Map 9   Ellsworth-Cherryfield

Schoodic Point

On a clear day, Schoodic Point provides an outstanding view of Mt. Desert Island and Frenchman Bay and is a photographer's delight. Two noteworthy plant species grow in the area. Healthy stands of Jack pine, which is uncommon in Maine, can be seen all along the peninsula. Black crowberry, an arctic species with tiny evergreen needles, grows luxuriantly in the parking lot at the point. Ducks, loons, and grebes winter offshore. Many eider nest on nearby islands, and mothers and chicks can be seen near the rocky shore in July and August. Pelagic birds are often blown inland by storms, and dovekies have been reported here and around Sorrento. Schoodic Point is an exposed outcrop of light-colored granite intruded by dark-colored basalt dikes.

Just past Ashville on US 1, follow signs for Schoodic Peninsula (Rte. 186). Schoodic Point is part of Acadia National Park. Free.

Blueberry Barrens

The Blueberry Barrens is a remarkable tundralike area officially known as Deblois Barrens. The expanse is underlain with glacial sediments which form numerous kettles, ridges, and outwash areas. A scattering of

Blueberry.

Crowberry.

tall red pine have grown on the sandy substrate, but the predominant cover is blueberry, a sturdy plant in the heath family which thrives on the nutrient-poor soil. Marsh hawk, upland sandpiper, savannah sparrow, vesper sparrow and bobolink regularly frequent the barrens. The area is privately owned and commercially cultivated for blueberries. (Nearby Cherryfield is the "blueberry capitol" of Maine.) The Blueberry Barrens are off the well-worn path, but it is worth driving through them just once to get a sense of the vast treeless land which lies hundreds of miles to the north.

From US 1 in Cherryfield, take Rte. 193 north 10.9 miles. Opposite a very small landing strip and left hand turn, take a right turn onto a dirt road. Bear right at the fork 1 mile past Great Falls Stream and continue 3 miles to Schoodic Lake. Return via the above route or follow the road as it circles north of the lake and then turns south to Cherryfield (stay right at the fork 2 miles south of Schoodic Lake). Free.

The Great Heath

The Great Heath is a large, undeveloped area of freshwater bog and forested peatland. Common bog plants such as sphagnum moss, leatherleaf, sheep laurel, bog rosemary, labrador tea, and rhodora—as well as several species of less common orchids—make up the largest heath in Maine. Northeast Peat Moss, Inc., which owns approximately one-third of the heath and has leased the other two-thirds from the state, estimates that eight million tons of dried peat moss can be mined from the area. Peat mining is relatively nonpolluting compared to other types of mining, but questions concerning conservation versus development have postponed major mining efforts.

The Great Heath is bisected by the Plesant River, a small, winding stream which rises in Pleasant Lake and eventually empties into the ocean. Canoeists generally allow a weekend for the trip, including time for birdwatching and botanizing in the heath and adjacent blueberry fields. The Pleasant River is unlike any other in Maine, for it combines secluded country with unique vegetation and provides a thoroughly enjoyable trip.

Details about canoeing the Pleasant River can be found in Maine canoeing guides. Public access to the Great Heath is primarily along the river. Free.

Cherryfield-Calais

Roque Bluffs Beach

Few beaches cling to the northern coast, which makes Roque Bluffs Beach all the more special. It is a pocket barrier beach which encloses a freshwater pond. The pond was probably once a marine lagoon before overwash and wind blocked the inlet. The beach face is steep and contains two rocky berms, correlating with the spring high tide and the neap high tide. Seabeach sandwort, beach pea, and American beachgrass are the dominant species. This may be the northernmost stand of beachgrass on the United States Atlantic coast, and it is certainly the northernmost recreational beach of any size on the mainland.

Just north of Jonesboro on US 1, turn south toward the town of Roque Bluffs. After 5 miles bear right for 2 miles. The road passes through the state park. Free.

Fort O'Brien

Fort O'Brien (or Fort Machias) overlooks Machias Bay. The large expanse of mudflats attracts many migrating shorebirds during late July, August, and September. Mountain cranberry, an arctic-alpine species, grows abundantly in the grass. Latitude, altitude, and the maritime effect (cool summers) influence the growth of arctic and alpine species. In this case, altitude is negligible, but the more northern latitude in conjunction with the maritime effect produce a good growing environment for mountain cranberry. Fort O'Brien was the site of the first naval battle of the Revolutionary War. The fort itself is no longer standing, and only breastworks remain. The area is a humble one, good for birdwalking and picnicking.

From US 1 in Machias, take Rte. 92 south for 5 miles. Free.

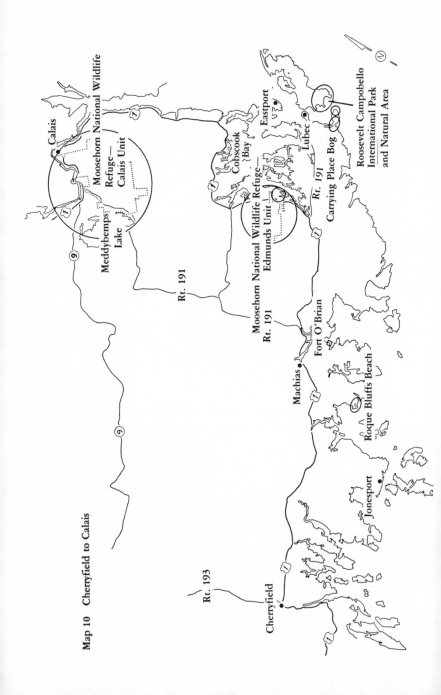

Map 10 Cherryfield to Calais

Calais

Moosehorn National Wildlife
Refuge—Calais Unit

Meddybemps
Lake

Rt. 191

Cobscook
Bay

Eastport

Lubec

Rt. 191

Carrying Place Bog

Roosevelt Campobello
International Park
and Natural Area

Moosehorn National Wildlife Refuge—
Edmunds Unit

Rt. 191

Fort O'Brian

Machias

Roque Bluffs Beach

Jonesport

Rt. 193

Cherryfield

Quoddy Head State Park

Wind-flagged spruce and bare limbs, stripped of needles by a relentless wind, bear evidence to the harsh life on an exposed coast. West Quoddy Head is a land of extremes. Twenty to twenty-eight foot tides wrack the coast, producing a huge swath of intertidal zone (superb for study of seaweeds and small marine creatures). The park is the easternmost point in the United States, and West Quoddy Light stands sentinal to the North Atlantic. Relatively few people visit this area, but those who do have a sense that they are, indeed, on the leading edge of the country.

A tiny path leads from the south end of the parking lot to the rocky shore. The trail continues for about a mile, crossing a bog just west of Green Point, the grassy peninsula, and skirting the shore. Eider can be seen all year, and ducks commonly winter offshore. The exciting area for birdwatching, however, is along the coastal flats between Lubec and West Quoddy Head. This is one of the two sites in the state where the rare curlew sandpiper has been seen, and it attracts thousands of common shorebirds each fall.

From US 1 in Whiting, take Rte. 189 north. Continue 4.1 miles past West Lubec and turn right at the sign for Quoddy. Travel 3.2 miles, bearing left at Carrying Place Cove, and continue to parking lot. Free.

Carrying Place Bog

Carrying Place Bog is the best example in the state of a raised bog. It was created by sphagnum moss, which grew, layer upon layer, until the bog had risen above the original ground level. It supports several arctic species, including baked apple berry and reindeer moss, and gives the feeling of barren land tundra. The area also supports a large stand of rhodora. The bog is being destroyed by violent northwesterly storms, and obvious erosion is occurring along the cobble beach. Carrying Place Bog is privately owned but can be observed from the road.

Follow directions for Quoddy Head. The bog is located on the northern side of the neck leading to West Quoddy Head. Free.

Moosehorn National Wildlife Refuge

Moosehorn National Wildlife Refuge was established in 1937 as one of a series of waterfowl preserves stretching from Maine to Florida. The refuge includes over 22,000 acres of woodland, ponds, bogs, and marsh. The mixed habitat ranges from post-burn to upland spruce-fir forest and supports a wide variety of flora and fauna. The refuge is composed

Woodcock.

of two separate areas, the Edmunds Unit on Cobscook Bay and the Calais Unit on the St. Croix River. Available at the visitor center are lists of birds, reptiles, amphibians, fish, and mammals, in addition to maps and other literature. Numerous hiking routes and a self-guided tour road (Calais Unit) cross the refuges. Cross-country skiing, skating, and snowshoeing are encouraged. Snowmobiling is permitted, although several trails are designated as skiing only.

Moosehorn is centered in the northeastern breeding range of the American woodcock. Extensive research has been conducted concerning habitat, nesting, food, and population management of the woodcock, as well as of waterfowl and geese. During the 1950s a flock of captive Canada geese were released in the marshes. These geese established a nesting population which produces about 50 birds annually. Over 130 bird species nest at Moosehorn, including the marsh hawk, which nests nowhere else in Maine.

Although parts of the refuge are managed for timber, two large sections totaling almost 7500 acres have been set aside as wilderness areas. Four sites are designated as "typical habitats" for research purposes: Sunken Meadows (woodcock), Bertrand Smith Natural Area (white

172

pine), Edmunds Unit Natural Area (red spruce) and Sunken Bog (Sphagnum bog).

Visitor Center is 3 ½ miles west of Calais on US 1. The refuge can also be reached by going north on Rte. 214. Free.

Cobscook Bay State Park

Cobscook Bay State Park is one of Maine's loveliest parks. "Cobscook" is Abenaki for "boiling tides," referring to the 24 to 28-foot tides which characterize the northern coastal stretch. The park is part of the Edmunds Unit of Moosehorn Refuge and contains rocky shore and woodland habitat. A map of the park and the Edmunds Unit are available at the park entrance. Numerous trails run throughout the area. Harbor seals are often seen basking on half-tide ledges and small islands. Harbor porpoise, which feed in shallow water during the summer, are occasionally spotted near the park.

From junction of US 1 and Rte. 189 in Whiting, travel north on US 1 for 4.2 miles to the sign for the state park. Fee: $ .75 per car.

Eastport

In the spring of 1833 John James Audubon traveled by mail coach and carriage to Eastport, where he boarded a schooner en route to Labrador. Before he left, he noted an abundance of "Bonapartian gulls" in the channel between Eastport and Deer Island, New Brunswick. Bonaparte's gulls still gather in this channel. From mid-August through mid-September, they congregate in the thousands, feeding on a multitude of shrimp which are carried to the surface by high tide currents around Deer Island. Herring gull, black-backed gull, kittiwake, and laughing gull are also common at this time, while glaucous gull and Iceland gull are often seen in the winter. Amid these regular visitors, rare species are sometimes seen. Sabine's gull, little gull, Franklin's gull, black-headed gull, and ivory gull have all been reported from Eastport. In addition, huge flocks of Northern phalarope gather to share the shrimp harvest. One estimate puts the number of phalaropes at two to three million birds in the channel at this time of year. The best view for birding can be gained by taking the ferry which runs between Eastport and Deer Island.

According to Indian legend, the islands in this area were created by the magic of great Chief Glooscap. As Glooscap paddled his canoe along the shores of Passamaquoddy Bay, he beheld a pack of wolves chasing a moose and a deer. When the wolves were about to move in for the kill, Glooscap lifted his hand and changed them all to islands. To-day, Moose Island (Eastport) and Deer Island sit side by side in Passama-quoddy Bay, while the Wolves Islands are still "moving in" a few miles offshore.

From US 1 in Perry, take Rte. 190 for 6 miles to Eastport. Free.

Raccoon.

Campobello Island, New Brunswick

Campobello Island is a unique area of northern boreal and tundra vegetation. Anyone interested in northern regions will be delighted with a visit to Campobello. Arctic and bog species grow well in the ex-posed heaths, wetlands, and plains. The island contains many miles of hiking trails and dirt roads. Roosevelt Campobello International Park and Natural Area, which encompasses the southern end of the island, includes the Roosevelt home. Natural history material and trails in the park are being developed.

Campobello is an excellent area for birdwatching. It is on the Atlantic Flyway and attracts many migrating land and sea birds. In addition, whales have been sighted from Head Harbor Light during the summer months. Maps and a short natural history description of both Campobello Island and the park itself are available at the park visitor center.

From US 1 in Whiting, take Rte. 189 for 12.2 miles to the Roosevelt Memorial Bridge. Free.

Appendix A

REPORTING SIGHTINGS OF RARE OR UNUSUAL ANIMALS

Bird Sightings

To report bird sightings, include date and time of day sighted, length of time observed, number of birds, adult/immature, behavior (soaring, feeding, perching, etc.), exact location, and observer's name and address.

Unusual birds: Maine Audubon Society
Gilsland Farm
118 Old Route One
Falmouth, Maine 04105

Bald eagles: Bald Eagle Project
Nutting Hall
University of Maine
Orono, Maine 04473

Unusual birds: The *Guillemot*
Box 373
Sorrento, Maine 04677

The *Guillemot* is an amateur bi-monthly newsletter, published by the Sorrento Scientific Society, concerning natural history in Maine. It includes interesting reports of mammals, reptiles, invertebrates, and plants as well as birds.

Whale Sightings

To report whale sightings, describe number seen, size, behavior, particular characteristics, location, and exact time. Send information to:

Allied Whale
College of the Atlantic
Bar Harbor, Maine 04609

Whale sighting forms may be obtained from Allied Whale.

Seal Sightings

Although seals are more commonly seen than whales, it is still important to monitor their numbers and location. Reports should include the same information as whale reports as well as wind speed, air temperature, sea state, and stage of the tide. Information can be sent to the above address or to:

David Richardson
Fisheries Research Station
West Boothbay Harbor, Maine 04575

Appendix B

STATE PARKS

The Bureau of Parks and Recreation has two pamphlets which list all of the state parks and historic sites, describe the facilities, and give exact dates of operation. These areas are usually officially open from Memorial Day until Labor Day but are available to the public at other times of the year. Fees indicated in the text are for adults; senior citizens and children are lower. Of the parks included in this book, only Bradbury Mountain, Camden Hills, and Cobscook Bay have camping facilities. For further information, write:

Bureau of Parks and Recreation
Maine Department of Conservation
Ray Building
Augusta, Maine 04333

Glossary of Ecological Terms

AEOLIAN FLAT: Flat, sparsely vegetated, windswept area in a dune field.

AVIFAUNA: Birdlife.

BACKSHORE: Area of beach extending from high water level to frontal dune ridge.

BACKWASH: Foamy water which washes down the beach face.

BARRIER BEACH: Beach which is attached to the mainland at both ends and protects a lagoon or former lagoon; may or may not include a tidal inlet.

BARRIER SPIT BEACH: Beach which extends part of the way across a bay mouth and is associated with a long, straight dune field, a tidal inlet, and a SALT MARSH.

BERM: Flat area of a beach extending from the mean high tide line to DUNES or rocky upland; usually the recreational area of a beach.

BOG: Poorly drained, nutrient deficient, acid wetland characterized by sphagnum, sedges, and HEATHS.

CARNIVORE: A flesh-eating animal or an insectivorous plant.

CUSPATE FORELAND: Seaward projection of beach and DUNE which often forms at one end of a TOMBOLO.

DECIDUOUS TREE: A tree which loses its leaves at the end of the growing period, usually once each year.

DELTA: A plain underlain by sediments that accumulate where a stream flows into a body of standing water where its velocity and transporting power are suddenly reduced.

DESICCATION: Drying by wind or heat.

DETRITUS: Disintegrated plant material.

DUNE: A hill or ridge of sand piled up by the wind.

ECOSYSTEM: A community of interacting animals, plants, and environment which forms a functioning whole in nature.

ERRATIC: Stone or boulder carried by ice to a place where it rests on or near bedrock of different composition.

ESKER: Long, narrow ridge of sand and gravel which was once the bed of a stream which ran in or beneath glacial ice.

FORAGE: To wander in search of food.

FORESHORE: Intertidal zone of a beach.

FRINGING BEACH: Beach which lies next to bedrock or soil and does not have an extensive dune field or interior lagoon.

GABBRO: A coarse-grained igneous rock with the composition of basalt; characteristically dark rock with deeply intermeshed crystals which make it very rough.

GEOMORPHIC: Relating to the form of the earth or its surface features.

GLACIER: Mass of ice formed by recrystallization of snow that flows forward by gravity.

GNEISS: Metamorphic rock commonly formed by metamorphism of granite; gneiss has banded structure due to separation of light and dark minerals by heat and pressure.

GRAYWACKE: Variety of sandstone characterized by hardness, dark color, and angular grains of quartz, feldspar, and small rock fragments set in clay-sized particles.

HABITAT: The place or type of environment where a plant or animal naturally lives.

HARDWOOD: Broad-leaved tree.

HEATH: BOG; a family of shrubby plants that thrives in a bog.

HIBERNATOR: An animal which passes the winter in a torpid or resting state.

IGNEOUS ROCK: Rock formed by the cooling and solidification of magma, either within the earth or on its surface.

KAME TERRACE: A level body of sand and gravel deposited by water running between a stagnant lobe of glacial ice and an adjacent valley wall.

KETTLEHOLE: Bowl-shaped depression formed by melting of large chunk of ice which was insulated by sand and gravel.

LAMINARIA: Genus name for large, chiefly perennial kelps with unbranched and often flat blades.

LITTORAL: Coastal.

MAGMA: Molten mixtures of minerals, often rich in gases.

MARSH: Wetland characterized by moving water and good nutrient supply consisting of grasses, sedges, and rushes but no trees.

METAMORPHIC ROCK: Rock changed in texture or composition by heat, pressure, or chemically active fluids.

MICA: A group of silicate minerals characterized by perfect sheet or scale cleavage resulting from their atomic pattern.

MIDDEN: A refuse heap, especially one composed of shells and bones which mark the site of a primitive human habitation.

MORAINE: Rock material brought forward to the outer edge of glacial ice and deposited in small or large ridges.

MUDFLAT: Salt flats or tidal flats which are covered twice a day with salt water.

NEAP TIDE: A tide of minimum range occurring at the first and third quarters of the moon.

NECK: A narrow stretch of land.

OFFSHORE: Area along a beach which is always covered with water.

OROGENY: Process of mountain formation.

OUTWASH PLAIN: Flat or gently sloping surface underlain by material carried from a glacier by meltwater.

PARABOLIC DUNE: U-shaped sand dune which can be blown down-wind.

PEGMATITE: A coarse-grained igneous rock with crystals which range from an inch to many feet in length.

PELAGIC: Associated with or pertaining to the open ocean.

PHOTOSYNTHESIS: Formation of carbohydrates in chlorophyll-containing tissues of plants exposed to light.

POCKET BEACH: Any beach which forms between two headlands; usually refers to small beach between nearby headlands.

PREDATOR: An animal that lives by killing and consuming other animals.

PREY: An animal which is taken by another animal as food.

PROMONTORY: Headland; high point of land or rock projecting into a body of water.

REACH: A continuous unbroken stretch of a stream or river.

REENTRANT: Tidal inlet containing sand deposited by wave action.

RHIZOME: Horizontal subterraneous plant stem that is often thickened by deposits of reserve food material; produces both shoots above and roots below.

RUNNEL: Tiny stream.

SALT MARSH: Wetland where the water is salt or brackish rather than fresh.

SALT PAN: A poorly drained area in the salt marsh which traps water; subsequent evaporation concentrates sea salt in this area.

SCARP: Low, steep slope along a beach caused by wave erosion.

SCAT: Droppings, dung.

SCHIST: A metamorphic rock dominated by fibrous or platy minerals.

SEDIMENTARY ROCK: Rock formed from accumulations of sediment (rock fragments, remains of animals or plants, products of chemical action or evaporation) characterized by stratification.

SHOAL: Shallow.

SOFTWOOD: Coniferous trees.

SPIT: A sandy bar built by currents into a bay from a headland.

SPRING TIDE: A tide of maximum range occurring at the new and full moon.

SUBSTRATE: The base, usually soil, on which an organism lives.

SUCCESSION: Orderly replacement of one plant community with another community as sunlight, water, and soil nutrient conditions change.

SWAMP: Wetland characterized by moving water and good nutrient supply consisting of trees, shrubs, and smaller plants.

SWASH: Foamy water which washes over the beach face after a wave has broken.

TECTONIC: Relating to the deformation of the earth's crust.

TIDAL POOL: Pool which has standing water at all times (only the depth changes with tide and evaporation).

TILL: Layer of rocks and rock particles which have been carried along in glacial ice and left behind when the ice melted.

TOMBOLO: Small beach or bar running between two islands or connecting one island with the mainland; may be exposed only at low tide.

TUNDRA: Level or undulating treeless plain characteristic of arctic regions.

Index

More Books by The East Woods Press

Hosteling USA—The Official American Youth Hostels Handbook
The Healthy Trail Food Book, by Dorcas S. Miller
The New England Guest House Book, by Corinne Madden Ross
Roxy's Ski Guide to New England, by Roxy Rothafel
Exploring Nova Scotia, by Lance Feild
Hiking Cape Cod, by John Mitchell and Whit Griswold
Berkshire Trails for Walking and Ski Touring, by Whit Griswold
Walks in the Catskills, by John Bennet and Seth Masia
Canoeing the Jersey Pine Barrens, by Robert Parnes
Hiking Virginia's National Forests, by Karin Wuertz-Schaefer
Tennessee Trails, by Evan Means
Trout Fishing the Southern Appalachians, by J. Wayne Fears
Rocky Mountain National Park Hiking Trails, by Kent & Donna Dannen